TOUGH
QUESTIONS
REVISED EDITION

TOUGH
QUESTIONS
LEADER'S
GUIDE

The Tough Questions Series

**TOUGH
QUESTIONS**
REVISED EDITION

TOUGH

QUESTIONS

LEADER'S

GUIDE

TOUGH QUESTIONS LEADER'S GUIDE

GARRY POOLE
&
JUDSON POLING

foreword by **Lee Strobel**

WILLOW CREEK RESOURCES

ZONDERVAN™

GRAND RAPIDS, MICHIGAN 49530 USA

We want to hear from you. Please send your comments about this book
to us in care of zreview@zondervan.com. Thank you.

ZONDERVAN™

Tough Questions Leader's Guide
Copyright © 1998, 2003 by Willow Creek Association

Requests for information should be addressed to:

Zondervan, *Grand Rapids, Michigan 49530*

ISBN 0-310-24509-5

Interior design by Nancy Wilson

Printed in the United States of America

03 04 05 06 07 08 09 /❖ CH/ 10 9 8 7 6 5 4 3 2 1

Contents

Foreword

For most of my life I was an atheist. I thought that the Bible was hopelessly riddled with mythology, that God was a man-made creation born of wishful thinking, and that the deity of Jesus was merely a product of legendary development. My no-nonsense education in journalism and law contributed to my skeptical viewpoint. In fact, just the idea of an all-powerful, all-loving, all-knowing creator of the universe seemed too absurd to even justify the time to investigate whether there could be any evidence backing it up.

However, my agnostic wife's conversion to Christianity, and the subsequent transformation of her character and values, prompted me to launch my own spiritual journey in 1980. Using the skills I developed as the legal affairs editor of *The Chicago Tribune,* I began to check out whether any concrete facts, historical data, or convincing logic supported the Christian faith. Looking back, I wish I had this curriculum to supplement my efforts.

This excellent material can help you in two ways. If you're already a Christ-follower, this series can provide answers to some of the tough questions your seeker friends are asking—or that you're asking yourself. If you're not yet following Christ but consider yourself either an open-minded skeptic or a spiritual seeker, this series can also help you in your journey. You can thoroughly and responsibly explore the relevant issues while discussing the topics in community with others. In short, it's a tremendous guide for people who really do want to discover the truth about God and this fascinating and challenging Nazarene carpenter named Jesus.

If the previous paragraph describes you in some way, prepare for the adventure of a lifetime. Let the pages that follow take you on a stimulating journey of discovery as you grapple with the most profound—and potentially life-changing—questions in the world.

—Lee Strobel, author of
The Case for Christ and *The Case for Faith*

Introduction

Welcome to the Leader's Guide for the Tough Questions series. We believe that leading a group to discuss and explore the tough spiritual questions in this set of guides will be well worth the time and effort you invest. This series will stretch you and your group members to consider questions outside everyone's comfort zones. But in so doing, you will guide your group to draw closer to discovering the truth about God and how to know him—and nothing could be more important than that!

What kinds of groups will want to delve into this study guide? In truth, both believers and seekers have these questions. And people from a wide spectrum of spiritual backgrounds and experiences will benefit from going through this series of discussions.

Sometimes people come to faith but later realize their foundation is shaky. You, along with other believers, may want to gain a better knowledge about the spiritual truths you've accepted for years. This curriculum will help reinforce your Christian foundation. Others are interested in this series because they have a spouse, relative, friend, or coworker who challenges them with tough questions. In this case, the guides can equip believers to engage in more productive and effective evangelistic discussions.

Still others are spiritual seekers—non-Christians investigating the claims of Christianity to determine whether they really are true. Because we recognize the need to provide a safe place for seekers to be heard and to get their objections and questions addressed, we've designed this series primarily for them. Whether your group includes only one or many seekers, we believe this material is a perfect fit for them to engage in such an exploration.

Training and preparation is essential, especially if you are leading a group of seekers. Too much is at stake to do otherwise. Prayerfully dedicate yourself to adequately preparing to facilitate great discussions that serve your group members well. Along with the information provided in this Leader's Guide, familiarize yourself with the introductory material of the study guide you use. That material will give you additional background information about the structure of this series. Carefully study the session you intend to cover and the corresponding Leader's Guide notes before the group meets. In most cases, your group members will also want to look over the lesson in advance, so always be sure to let them all know which one will be discussed next. It is also important for you to identify another Christian leader to serve as your apprentice. The two of you can provide support and feedback for each other as you facilitate group discussions and develop your leadership skills.

Because this series is mainly designed to assist groups of spiritual seekers to take steps in their journey toward Christ, we strongly recommend *Seeker Small Groups* as a companion volume to facilitating these discussions. This book thoroughly examines the principles and skills needed to effectively lead seeker small groups and serves as a helpful resource as you launch your group. In addition, we suggest you use the following tools to develop your evangelistic effectiveness as a seeker small group leader:

1. *The Three Habits of Highly Contagious Christians,* a discussion guide consisting of three sessions specifically designed for small groups of believers, to discuss and implement practical ways to reach out to seekers
2. *Becoming a Contagious Christian Course,* an excellent, in-depth evangelism training tool

Facilitating the Discussions

We chose a group format to explore these tough questions, mainly because people learn best in active discussion. It's interesting to note, as one reads the accounts of Jesus' life, how many times he stopped and asked people questions. Of course he had a message to convey, but he also knew that people listen *best* when they are first listened to. Dialogue honors seekers and awakens their minds. It shakes out theories and beliefs that seem plausible at first glance and holds them up to the light of careful scrutiny. Through this process, people are more likely to identify their own erroneous ideas and give up weak arguments in favor of verifiable ones.

As you prepare to use these guides, think through a sequence that would best serve your group. For example, while some groups would benefit from going through each of the seven books in a row, other groups might want to tailor the curriculum to better fit their needs, by selecting the one or two books that more closely fit their most pressing questions and issues. Since the series does not necessarily need to be discussed sequentially, the sessions can be mixed and matched in any order, based on your group members' interests and needs. So other groups may even want to identify and discuss several individual sessions from the entire series without being locked into any one book. In any case, we highly recommend that you link whatever you do with the guide *Why Become a Christian?* Always plan to incorporate discussions from this particular guide because of its strong emphasis on helping participants cross the line of faith and receive Christ as forgiver and leader.

Whatever the profile of your group, consider these cautions: First, it is important that you and your group members have realistic expectations. These guides do not cover every conceivable tough question, and you can't possibly answer in complete detail even the questions they do explore. While the guides can help you and your group members make great strides toward finding satisfying answers, studying these issues is a lifetime endeavor. Additional reading and Bible study will almost certainly be required for anyone to feel confident of his or her answers to any of these questions.

Group members may well be left with additional questions at the end of any one discussion. This may be somewhat disconcerting, but hopefully, with your encouragement, the group will maintain the process of ongoing questioning and learning. Try not to succumb to any pressure to end sessions by tying up loose ends with standard answers that don't really satisfy; instead let the searching progress throughout your group meetings (and beyond). Let your group members know from the onset that the discussions will help them to take steps in their spiritual journeys, but they won't necessarily receive nice and tidy answers to all their questions.

Second, we firmly believe in a process that honors people where they are right now—even if they have "wrong" responses. People need to know that within your group they will be respected and accepted no matter what, even if their beliefs are unorthodox. Inaccurate answers need to be heard, in part for comparison purposes but also because we should value one another. Paradoxically, when people feel the freedom to disclose their honest opinions, they become more open to hear what others have to say and gain a new appreciation for the answers provided to us by God in his Word. Our experience has shown us that people change their minds more readily when they are first invited to express themselves. This kind of treatment puts everyone in a position to freely explore other options.

Third, we believe that your group should go beyond the purely academic. If all you do is talk about questions and answers without also entering into a sense of community with the other group members, you will miss an important, life-changing dynamic. That is particularly true if you have seekers in your group. We've observed that people are more often repelled by Christianity because of the way they've been treated by Christians than by any inadequate answers they've heard from those believers. While this is a generalization, we believe the Tough Questions series provides a tremendous opportunity for seekers to receive a taste of a loving, caring community as well as solid answers. These are powerful tools in the Holy Spirit's arsenal to win back wandering souls. As the leader, set the relational temperature for your group—make it feel more like a family than a class.

Finally, we caution leaders against adopting a know-it-all attitude. People have joined your group to discuss and explore spiritual questions. Resist the temptation to teach and instead lead a process of discovery. You don't have to supply all the "correct" answers, and it will be better for all concerned if each person gets a chance to have his or her say. Over time, significant answers will begin to emerge from the collective discussion rather than from the knowledge of any one person in the group.

Study Guide Features

The Introduction

At the beginning of every session is an introduction, usually several paragraphs long. Some group members will read this beforehand, but we recommend also taking time to read it together at the beginning of every meeting. We suggest that you vary how this is done. One time, have an individual read it aloud; at another meeting, all members can read it silently. Or go around the circle and have each member read a paragraph.

The introductions are written from a skeptical point of view. If you're leading a seeker group, you'll most likely have skeptics in your group, so these readings will help them feel understood and valued. This information should also help the believers in your group to feel the force of the tough questions seekers ask. Most Christians have known someone who has raised similar questions, and many have even raised them themselves. The introductions are also intended to be provocative. These are, after all, tough questions, and people should squirm a little when they face them.

Open for Discussion

Following the introductions, you'll find the core of the session: the questions. Don't insist that everyone answer every question, because some people may feel uneasy or put on the spot. Encourage those who want to respond to do so, but also be sensitive to those who are quiet. Help draw reserved members into the discussion—without being threatening. Usually, as the quieter ones begin to see that you accept those with differing opinions, they will gradually join in the discussion.

Most sessions contain ten to fifteen questions. It may be difficult for your group to get through all of them in one sitting. That's okay; the important thing is to engage group members in the topic at hand. Your group may decide to spend more than one meeting on each session in order to more thoroughly tackle all of the questions. There are two extremes that leaders must help their groups avoid. The first is a regimented attempt to complete every question, as if the session were an end in itself. The second is to allow the group to get too far off on tangents and not get to the real issues they are there to discuss.

These questions are designed to draw people out and to give them the opportunity to grapple with spiritual issues out loud. As a leader, your role is to facilitate that "self-discovery" process. So be careful not to short-circuit the learning process by giving quick answers to difficult questions. Instead, let people live with the tension of those unanswered questions and eventually you will lead them to embrace satisfying answers that they discover on their own.

People need to wrestle deep in their souls with the significant questions—not just the superficial ones. Whatever you can do as a leader to draw out those deeper issues and engage everyone in those discussions will have a valuable impact on the whole group.

First Question

Usually the first question of each session is an "icebreaker." These simple questions are designed to get the conversation going by prompting the group to discuss a nonthreatening issue, generally one having to do with the session topic to be covered. Starting with a lighthearted, "personal interest" question helps people bridge the gap between what's going on in their lives and what will happen in the group meeting. You may want to make time for additional icebreakers at the beginning of each discussion. If so, *The Complete Book of Questions: 1001 Conversation Starters for Any Occasion* is filled with icebreaker questions designed for this purpose. Extended interactions will draw your group members closer together as they spend quality time getting to know each other.

Heart of the Matter

The section called "Heart of the Matter" represents a slight turn in the group discussion. Generally speaking, the questions in this section speak more to the emotional, rather than just the intellectual, side of the issue. Part of the philosophy behind the Tough Questions series is the recognition that people have emotional as well as intellectual needs. God can and does meet both. As a leader, you should attempt to guide your group members to discover satisfying answers for both their hearts and their minds.

Charting Your Journey

The purpose of "Charting Your Journey" is to help group members go one step beyond a mere intellectual and emotional discussion to personal application. Group members' views will inevitably change over the course of time, and one of the greatest rewards of leading these discussions will be to see that progress.

Straight Talk

Every session has at least one section, called "Straight Talk," designed to stimulate further thinking and discussion around relevant supplementary information. Again, try to use a variety of approaches for reading these aloud in the group meeting. The question immediately following a Straight Talk usually refers to the material just presented, so it is important that group members read and understand this part before they attempt to answer the question.

Quotes

Scattered throughout every session are various quotes, many of them from skeptical or critical points of view. These are intended to enhance the reader's thinking but are not necessary to address the session's questions.

Scripture for Further Study

In most guides, each session ends with a list of suggested Scripture passages to reflect on that relate to the discussion topic.

Recommended Resources

This section at the back of each guide lists recommended books that may serve as helpful resources for further study.

Leader's Guide Notes

The material provided in this Leader's Guide corresponds to every session in each of the seven books. These notes are intended to give you insights behind the inclusion of particular questions as well as to supply you with suggested responses from a Christian perspective. Read through them as you prepare to facilitate your group discussions.

Short Answer

Each session in the Leader's Guide begins with a "Short Answer." This is usually a one-sentence summary of the conclusion we hope seekers will discover as they discuss the topic. Reading this Short Answer out loud to the group is *not* recommended, since it might very well short-circuit the discovery process. Rather this Short Answer is intended to give you, as the leader, an idea of the direction the session will hopefully take.

Comments

For your convenience, all the questions in each of the seven discussion guides are listed in this Leader's Guide. Not all the questions include notes, however, because explanations are not always necessary. As you prepare for your meeting, study these comments to better understand the general responses you hope to elicit from the group. If possible try to lead the dialogue along these lines. You may also want to use the notes as a guide for articulating your responses to some of the questions, if they accurately reflect your position. As with the Short Answers, we do *not* recommend simply reading the Leader's Guide comments to the group. Let the group make these discoveries in their own time—the impact will be greater and longer lasting!

We believe that you, as the leader, are on as great an adventure as that of the people in your group. We encourage you to pray for each participant and to pray for guidance and wisdom as you stretch your own limits of leadership and learning. Without you, this group wouldn't happen, so it's our hope and prayer that you'll sense God's hand on you as you step into this role. May his power make your Tough Questions group a place where truth and love meet in perfect proportions. God bless you on this life-changing journey!

CHAPTER ONE

How Does Anyone Know God Exists?

DISCUSSION ONE

Is Anybody Out There?

Short Answer: Yes! Not only is God out there, he is personal, he cares, and he is reaching out to you.

Question 1: Think back to your childhood. What did you believe about God during those years? Describe some ways your views have changed since then.

Question 2: What are some factors that have influenced your current beliefs about God? One of the most significant factors affecting our view of God is the image of our parents—whether good or bad. Things they said or didn't say and did or didn't do probably made an impact on us that lasts to this day. Another notable influence might be respected (or otherwise) authority figures. Peer pressure may also have contributed to our thinking about God, as well as things we observe in nature, books, and other information we have gathered from people we hold in high regard. Our consciences also tell us something about God.

There are at least two reasons why these questions are included here: the first is to enable you and your group members to learn more about each other; the second, to build bridges of trust between the members of the group. It is important for group members to develop and maintain respect for each other, regardless of where they are in their spiritual journeys.

Question 3: Which of the above positions [see guide] about God represents the most common belief among people you know? Which view is least popular among your friends and acquaintances? Give reasons for your answers.

Question 4: How convinced are your friends and acquaintances that their views and beliefs about God are accurate? What do you think determines the level of confidence they have?

Question 5: How do you think people decide what they're going to believe about God? What do you think they base their beliefs about God upon? Many people are unintentional or haphazard in how they arrive at their view about God. It is important for us to see the reasons behind what we believe. This question can help people see (maybe for the first time) that most individuals don't have substantial reasons to back up what they believe about God.

Question 6: Which of the views of God listed makes the most sense to you? Why? Make sure to withhold any judgment or condemnation toward those who may not believe as you do. It's very important to offer unconditional acceptance toward everyone in your group.

Question 7: On a scale from one to ten (one represents low confidence and ten represents high confidence), how certain are you that your view is based on actual evidence rather than opinion? In many cases, this will be the very first time group members will have ever been asked to identify and describe their confidence level about what they believe. This may make some uncomfortable. Still, part of building a good foundation for belief is to recognize the crumbling concrete of an existing spiritual foundation so there will eventually be a new readiness to find a way to build a stronger one. It is important for members to feel the freedom and safety to share their true thoughts and uncertainties in the group and not feel judged or put down in any way for what they do or don't believe. In his book *Asking God Your Hardest Questions*, Lloyd Ogilvie, onetime chaplain of the U.S. Senate, asserts, "Johann Wolfgang von

Goethe once said, 'Give me the benefit of your convictions, if you have any, but keep your doubts to yourself, for I have enough of my own.' I don't agree with that. I want to put it differently: Give me your doubts. Be honest enough to admit them. Our Lord is pressing us on to new growth. Our doubt is our human response. He can take our struggle with doubt and give us the gift of faith to ask for wisdom." That's exactly what you want to do in your group discussion—invite people to openly and honestly express their doubts and uncertainties. The first step in overcoming disbelief is identifying it.

Question 8: **What might help to increase the level of confidence you have in what you believe about God? Explain.**

Question 9: **What other specific examples can you give of "everyday faith"?** The point of this question is to help group members see that they exercise faith all the time, not just in spiritual matters. Every day people put their trust in things without taking much time to assess the trustworthiness of the objects of their confidence. What makes trusting God difficult is that God is not tangible, whereas these everyday things are. R. C. Sproul, in his book *Now, That's a Good Question,* states, "I don't think there's anything that makes living the Christian life more difficult than the fact that the Lord we serve is invisible to us. You know the expression in our culture 'Out of sight, out of mind.' It's very, very difficult to live your life dedicated to someone or something you cannot see. Often you hear people say that when they can see it, taste it, touch it, or smell it, they'll believe and embrace it, but not before. This is one of the most difficult problems of the Christian life: God is rarely perceived through our physical senses." But God does give reliable evidence of his existence and trustworthiness, and this series is about discovering that evidence.

Question 10: **During those times when absolute proof is impossible (there is no guarantee a plane will arrive safely), what factors help you determine whether you'll place your trust in something?** Possible answers include the reputation of the person or company you are trusting (i.e., credentials, training, title, research, appearances, past experiences, recommendations). Note: Lack of trust is based on these same factors.

Question 11: **What factors would help you get to reasonable certainty concerning God's existence?** Many of us assume that if God were to show up somewhere and speak to us, then we would believe. Others might want answers to prayers, and other signs that God is showing them favor. Intellectual types may ask for historical evidence or scientific proof. Note: As a leader, be sure not to belittle the responses you hear, no matter how foolish or inadequate the answers may seem.

Question 12: **Check the statement(s) below [see guide] that best describes your position at this point. Share your selection with the rest of the group and give reasons for your response.**

DISCUSSION TWO

How Can Anyone Be Sure God Exists?

Short Answer: We may not be able to have *absolute* certainty, but we may have *reasonable* certainty.

Question 1: **Give an example or two of something you place your trust in even though you are unable to perceive it with your five senses.**

Question 2: **What is one thing you no longer believe today that you believed when you were younger? What changed your mind?**

Question 3: **Share some of the concrete reasons you have now for your belief—or disbelief—in the existence of God.** Press your group members to go beyond describing influences to giving concrete reasons that could persuade someone else to adopt their point of view. As we pointed out in the previous session, people tend not to have compelling reasons for their beliefs—they usually believe the way they do without stopping to examine why.

Question 4: **Do you believe the sun will rise tomorrow? Why or why not? Can you provide proof for your response?**

Question 5: **How does this reality [see guide] impact your ability or inability to believe in God?** For those who are concerned with proving God "scientifically," this question can help reveal that the realm of science can't conclusively address the question.

Question 6: **What arguments other than those above [see guide] might people give against the existence of God?**

Question 7: **To what extent do these arguments and other factors influence your own thinking that God may not exist? Explain.** Do not feel pressured to address all the issues raised as a result of this question. At this point just let group members express their doubts and questions.

Question 8: **Select the argument [see guide] that for you is the strongest support of the existence of God. Which is the weakest argument? Give reasons for your selections.** Don't get sidetracked or bogged down by this question. Experience shows that these arguments don't completely make or break someone's belief or disbelief in God. They are helpful but often not conclusive.

Question 9: **Do you think most people consider the above arguments (for and against) when drawing a conclusion about the existence of God? Why or why not? Should they?** For some the identified arguments are helpful, but for others questions will still remain.

Question 10: **Why do you think Jesus said that people who do not see and yet still believe will be blessed?** One possibility is that such people demonstrate that they have a healthy balance between weighing the existing evidence and trusting God, without being plagued by ongoing doubt. God does not commend gullibility, but placing one's trust in

God can lead to contentment and a secure relationship with him.

Question 11: **There probably isn't a person alive who hasn't had doubts about the existence of God. When have you experienced these doubts, and how have you dealt with them?**

Question 12: **Does this experiment [see guide] seem reasonable to you? Is this something you would be open to trying sometime? Why or why not?** This exercise might seem threatening to some group members. Do not make them feel obligated to try it. Simply encourage each person to be open to the possibility.

Question 13: **What are your fears about God and what he might be like? How do you think those fears affect your confidence in his existence, or your ability to trust him?** One of the main reasons people struggle with God is the terrifying view they've adopted of him. As the group leader, one of your tasks is to help people see the God who is really there, not the God of their fears. The next session will address our distorted views of God and try to give a clearer picture of him, which should provide some comfort and hope to your group members. "Because God has spoken and has revealed himself, we no longer have the need or the option of conjuring up ideas and images of God by our own imaginations. Our personal concept of God—when we pray, for instance—is *worthless* unless it coincides with his revelation of *himself*" (Paul Little, *Know What You Believe*).

Question 14: **Check the statement(s) below [see guide] that best describes your position at this point. Share your selection with the rest of the group and give reasons for your response.**

DISCUSSION THREE

What Is God Really Like?

Short Answer: God is better than you ever imaged him to be, and the clearest picture of him is Jesus.

Question 1: Imagine you are taking a survey, asking people what they think God is like. What are the most common characteristics they would mention?

Question 2: Which of the three images of God mentioned in the introduction (grandfather, policeman, mechanic) most closely resembles your own understanding of God? What circumstances in your past have contributed to that image of him? This question, and the one following, can help you learn more about the people in your group and where they are coming from, spiritually speaking. This information can be helpful as you encourage them on their spiritual journeys.

Question 3: Which of the attributes listed above [see guide] grab your attention more than the others? Explain why those characteristics stand out for you.

Question 4: As you examine the above list [see guide], are there any attributes that surprise or confuse you? Which ones and why?

Question 5: Given the above list of God's attributes [see guide], does God seem appealing to you? Why or why not? To what degree would you like to get to know God better? The enthusiasm a person feels toward the idea of getting to know God is dependent on what that person knows or believes about God's attributes: is he someone the person would enjoy knowing? Also of concern is what a person feels God would provide: what needs might he meet or what benefits will he bring? This may sound selfish but it's probably an accurate gauge of the primary motivation behind a person's search for God. A. W. Tozer once said, "What we believe about God is the most important thing about us."

Question 6: Fill in this blank [see guide] with words you've heard or said yourself. What's your reaction to the thinking behind such statements?

Question 7: Do you agree with this statement [see guide]? Why or why not? The feathers in the analogy represent our opinions, which are weak (featherweight), while we mistake them to be strong (solid, reliable). The wind (reality, truth), not the feathers, has the power. Many people consider their opinions to determine truth, when in fact truth stays the same regardless of our opinions.

Question 8: **Now, using the spokes of the wheel below [see guide], explain what your life could be like if you really accepted God for all that he is and allowed him to demonstrate that attribute toward you in each area of your life.**

Question 9: **What do you suppose is missing from the devil's position about God? How is it possible to believe intellectually that God exists but then live as though he does not exist?** Honoring God as God means loving and obeying him. Be sensitive to those who might recognize that they are not living in a way that honors God. This question is not meant to be judgmental or make anyone feel bad but to expose faulty confidences; it is geared toward helping people discover that believing in God is not enough. Don't try to artificially ease the tension if your group members recognize the distance that exists between themselves and God.

Question 10: **Expand on what you think is meant by the following statement: "It's one thing to believe that the God described in the Bible exists, and quite another to let that belief impact your life." Do you agree with this statement? Why or why not?** This question is designed to continue the dialogue started in question 9. It goes a step further, making it more personal.

Question 11: **What is your greatest fear about what you'd be like and the changes that would take place if God were leading your life?** This question is similar to question 13 from the previous session, but it focuses on the changes that are presumed to occur if the person becomes a follower of Christ. Many people have an exaggerated or distorted view of what Christians are like, and are fearful of becoming one of "them."

Question 12: **Check the statement(s) below [see guide] that best describes your position at this point. Share your selec-**

tion with the rest of the group and give reasons for your response.

DISCUSSION FOUR

How Can Rational People Believe in Miracles?

Short Answer: A God who created everything is a God who can do miracles. The whole question of miracles hinges on the question of the existence of God.

Question 1: Which of these events [see guide] would you label as a miracle? Why?

Question 2: Why do you suppose many people find it difficult, if not impossible, to believe in miracles?

Question 3: What do you think of the following statement: **"If God doesn't exist, by definition miracles don't happen, because a miracle is an act of God. If, on the other hand, God does exist and he is the creator of the universe, miracles are possible because the God who created everything has the power to choose to do something else."** People who refuse to acknowledge the possibility of miracles may not claim to be atheists, but by denying this aspect of God's power, they accept a drastically altered picture of God. They may end up living like atheists, because they believe God doesn't get involved. Deists, for example, acknowledge God but believe he does not act in the world. Such a view is certainly not true of the God of the Bible. Paul Little, in his book *How to Give Away Your Faith,* answers the question of miracles this way: "The real issue is whether or not God exists. If God exists, then miracles are logical and pose no intellectual contradictions. A friend of mine who grew up in Asia once told me he just couldn't quite believe that a man could become God. I saw his problem in a flash and said, 'I'd have quite a time believing that, too. But I can easily believe that God became man.' There's all the difference in the world between these two concepts. By definition God is all-powerful. He can and does intervene in the universe that he has created."

Question 4: **Why would Paul make a point of noting the eyewitnesses who saw Jesus back from the dead? Why would the mention of five hundred people who simultaneously saw Jesus be a powerful piece of evidence?** Christianity is a religion grounded in events that actually occurred. Believing in something as unusual as a resurrection requires extraordinary support; therefore eyewitnesses help authenticate Christian belief. Multiple eyewitnesses give that much more credibility. Those who would explain the resurrection as a hallucination must explain how five hundred people could have had the same hallucination simultaneously.

Question 5: **According to these passages [see guide], what is the value of Jesus' miracles? Even though we are twenty centuries removed from the events, how is his point still valid?** God uses miracles to draw people to the person of Jesus. They are not common in our life, but they validate the extraordinary Son of God. Even though we are twenty centuries removed from Jesus' miracles, their "sign value"—the way they continue to point to Jesus' divinity and uniqueness—still underscores his incredible life.

Question 6: **Have you ever had a personal experience that you believe to be a miracle? Tell your group about that experience.** Your group members will probably describe unusual or unique experiences. It may be interesting to explore what the evidence is that their experiences were genuine miracles instead of just extraordinary (but not divine) occurrences.

Question 7: **What is your emotional reaction to the thought that God might do something in your life that you couldn't explain? What about the idea that he could do something miraculous for you, but hasn't?** The thought of miracles is really quite frightening. Many times when an angel appears to a person, the very first words heard are "Fear not." True miracles create fear. Regarding the second part of the question, people may feel anger or sadness because they desperately want God's intervention in their lives but haven't received it the way they had hoped. Assure group members that it is perfectly natural to be emotional about God's apparent indifference.

Question 8: What insight can you gain into human nature (and the limits of a miracle's ability to convince a biased heart) from this irrational reaction to Jesus' miracles? If a person is determined not to believe no matter what, a miracle won't change his or her mind.

Question 9: What specific questions about Christianity have you struggled with (in the past or now) that relate to the issue of miracles?

Question 10: Do you agree with the statement "If miracles never happen, Christianity cannot be true"? Explain. The whole basis of Christianity is the Resurrection, which is essentially a miracle.

Question 11: Check the statement(s) below [see guide] that best describes your position at this point. Share your selection with the rest of the group and give reasons for your response.

DISCUSSION FIVE

Does God Care About What Happens to Us?

Short Answer: Yes, so much so that he sent Jesus to bring hope and meaning into our world of hopelessness and despair.

Question 1: Describe a situation in which you misplaced or lost something very valuable. What did you do? How did that loss make you feel? How did you react when you finally discovered the valuable item for which you were looking? (If you never did find it, how did you react when you finally realized it was gone forever?)

Question 2: To what extent do you feel God cares about you and your life? Explain.

Question 3: What attitude is Jesus responding to when he begins to tell this parable [see guide]? Jesus is telling the story in response to the Pharisees' disapproval of Jesus' desire to be with "sinners."

Question 4: Do you suppose this woman was greedy[see guide]? What additional motive could have been behind her frantic search? Don't take a lot of time on these questions; the real punch comes when you discuss questions 5, 6, and 7.

Question 5: The two main elements in each parable symbolize the same two things. What is the common thread that binds these parables together? In other words, what do you suppose the two main elements in each parable represent?

- parable 1 elements: shepherd and sheep
- parable 2 elements: woman and coins
- parable 3 elements: father and son

  A. The first element (shepherd, woman, and father) represents God.
  B. The second element (sheep, coins, and son) represents people.

Question 6: Describe the reaction common to all three stories when the missing valuable was finally found.

Question 7: According to Jesus, what do these three stories teach concerning how much God values lost people? How then would you suppose God reacts when lost people come to him?

Question 8: How does your reaction in that situation compare with how God must feel toward those who are not yet part of his family?

Question 9: How do you feel about the idea that God hosts a heavenly celebration when a single person like you comes to him and is found?

Question 10: Read Matthew 6:25–26 and Matthew 10:29–31. What points in these verses are easy for you to accept? What points are difficult for you to agree with? Be sure to have these passages earmarked before the meeting and have someone read them out loud.

Question 11: **How difficult is it for you to really sense God's love for you personally? What factors influence this ability? Describe times in your life when you have felt loved by God.** God's love is constant, but that doesn't mean we always feel it. Guilt can make us feel unloved, as can seasons of pain or confusion, but God's love is still there. Our subjective experience of his love is not the same thing as the reality of his never-ending love. In his book *Give Me an Answer,* Cliffe Knechtle notes, "The wonderful promise of Scripture is that God is bigger than anything we can do that's wrong. God can reach deeper than any pit we can dig for ourselves. We cannot commit a sin that God cannot forgive."

Question 12: **What would God need to do in order for you to feel loved by him? What is your understanding of what he has done already?** Christians sometimes make it sound as if God were a vending machine: "I'll ask for this and he will respond accordingly and then I will feel loved." The reality is that God does do wonderful things for us, but he provides blessings that are more enduring, such as the forgiveness of sin and the promise of heaven. His love is not contingent on our getting our every wish granted. At this point in the discussion, you may have an opportunity to more fully explain the gospel message to your group.

Question 13: **On a scale from one to ten, place an X near the spot and phrase [see guide] that best describes you. Share your selection with the rest of the group and give reasons for placing your X where you did.**

DISCUSSION SIX

How Can a Person Get to Know God?

Short Answer: We come to know God by recognizing and receiving the way of salvation he's provided through his Son, Jesus Christ.

Question 1: Describe a situation in which you admired someone from a distance and then had an opportunity to meet and get to know the person. How did your perspective change concerning the person?

Question 2: Do you know people who believe they have encountered God in a way that is more significant and personal than merely knowing facts about him? What do you suppose they mean by this? In a group in which there are a number of seekers, this question will allow them to talk about their experiences (positive or negative) when they have interacted with Christians. This question also gets at the idea that there is a difference between concluding that God exists (which is an intellectual matter) and getting to know him personally (which goes beyond mere knowledge about God to actually encountering God through his Son, Jesus Christ).

Question 3: What do you think causes the barrier that seems to exist between God and people? Read Isaiah 59:1–2. According to this passage, what causes a separation between God and us? Why does this form such an impenetrable barrier? The barrier is not an informational barrier; it is a sin barrier.

Question 4: What does this verse [see guide] say about how God feels toward people who have shunned him and are therefore separated from him? God deeply loves those who are running away from him. The fact that we have shunned him has not stopped him from loving us. In fact, his great love for us took him a step further than mere words—he initiated a redemption plan.

Question 5: What is the biblical consequence associated with this gap [see guide] between God and us? Expand on what that might mean in everyday life (not just at the end of life). It is about being lost and experiencing the void, even though you are physically alive. It means living in a spiritually dead state. People who live life without God are missing out on true fulfillment in this life and in the life to come.

Question 6: According to these verses [see guide], what did God do to overcome the distance between people and himself?

Question 7: What does Jesus say eternal life is really all about? What does it mean to "know" God and Jesus Christ? In John 17:3 eternal life is defined as knowing God and Jesus Christ. Jesus is explaining that there is no eternal life without a relationship with God. And that can only happen through knowing Jesus Christ. To know Jesus in this sense is to place your faith and trust in him and maintain a deep, intimate relationship with him. For more commentary on this subject, see *Why Become a Christian,* discussion 1, question 6 in this Leader's Guide.

Question 8: To what extent do you feel you need to encounter God and know him on a deep personal level?

Question 9: What factors do you think influence a person to make a complete turnaround in what he or she believes spiritually? A wide variety of factors can motivate a person to be open to making dramatic changes in his or her life. But spiritual life, like biological life, must be nurtured and cultivated. Spirituality thrives in an atmosphere that contains such things as living in community (small groups), honestly facing doubts, learning more about God and his Word (the Bible), and conversing regularly with God (prayer).

Question 10: Describe an experience in which God was very real to you (if you have had such an experience). Ralph Waldo Emerson described the impact of God's creation on him when he stated, "All I have seen teaches me to trust the Creator for all I have not seen."

Question 11: How does this information [see guide] differ from what you have believed (now or in the past) concerning how a person can know God personally? What barriers prevent you from taking this kind of step toward God? Most religious training has taught people lists of rules to keep, behaviors that God wants, or the importance of holding correct beliefs about God. That teaching doesn't help them to see that God wants a day-to-day relationship with them. For others, religious life was an automatic thing, whether they wanted it or not; they were never taught about the need for a conscious, deliberate decision to receive Christ.

Question 12: **Now that we're at the end of this discussion guide, at what point would you describe yourself in your spiritual journey? On a scale from one to ten, place an *X* near the spot and phrase [see guide] that best describes you and where you are now. Share your selection with the rest of the group and give reasons for placing your *X* where you did.**

CHAPTER TWO

What Difference Does Jesus Make?

DISCUSSION ONE

Who Was Jesus?

Short Answer: Jesus is the most unique man who has ever lived, the Son of God, Savior of the world.

Question 1: What are some of the common things you have heard people say about who Jesus was?

Question 2: From the list of words and phrases below [see guide], check the top three that sum up your current understanding of Jesus.

Question 3: What is one word or phrase from the above list [see guide] that you believe is not true about Jesus?

Question 4: Which of the following [see guide] have strongly influenced your picture about who Jesus is?

Question 5: What are the strengths and weaknesses of relying on these sources [see guide]? People rarely think about why they believe what they believe about Jesus. Failing to critically examine the sources that have led to opinions is as dangerous as never examining those opinions. The reality is that many of us have based our eternal destiny on very precarious sources of information, and though our opinions might be strongly held, they are often weakly supported. Even though this question may expose group members' weak positions, be careful not to allow members of your group to express negative judgments of each other.

Encourage members to accept one another in spite of differences in beliefs.

Question 6: **Write a concise statement of Jesus' belief, based on information gleaned from the following passages [see guide].** One of the ways to see how striking Jesus' claims are is to imagine someone you know saying the same things. You would be very uncomfortable indeed to hear a friend, coworker, or even the minister of a local church make these incredible claims. As P. T. Forsyth noted, "These claims in a mere man would be egoism carried even to imperial megalomania" *(This Life and the Next).* Yet Jesus was the supreme model of meekness and self-sacrifice. In his book *Basic Christianity,* John R. W. Stott claims, "The most remarkable feature of all this self-centered teaching is that it was uttered by one who insisted on humility in others. He rebuked his disciples for their self-seeking and was wearied by their desire to be great. Did he not practice what he preached?"

Some of the conclusions you could draw out of these verses include:

- He said God won't accept you unless you accept him (Jesus).
- He said he has to be more important to you than even your most intimate family relationships.
- He said you have to love him even more than you love your own life.
- He said he was on equal footing with God, being over the Sabbath requirements (like God) rather than subject to them.
- He claimed to have existed before Abraham, using the phrase "I am" (not the expected "I was"), which was a term God used (see Exodus 3:14).
- He said that if you'd seen him, you'd seen God.
- He categorically admitted at his trial that he was the Messiah and the Son of God.

Question 7: **What is the strongest reason you can give for modifying or even rejecting the statements Jesus made** about himself? In other words, if you believe he was wrong, why was he wrong? What would be your more accurate description of Jesus' true identity? On what basis do people think they know better who Jesus was, two thousand years after the fact, than the eyewitnesses who spoke to him or to those who knew him? The audacity of modern people willing to rewrite the story of Jesus with absolutely no factual basis is astonishing! (Malcolm Muggeridge notes, "It is not that people believe in nothing—which would be bad enough—but that they believe in anything—which is really terrible.") This question will hopefully show any group members who are doing this that they really have no evidence for reworking Jesus' claims other than their subjective personal prejudice. (Simply allow this question and the answers given to help group members discover this about themselves.)

Question 8: **What do you think of this allegation [see guide] in light of what you've learned in this session?** People resisted what Jesus said about himself. Even his followers struggled with understanding exactly who he was. That he asserted his unique role and identity in so many and various ways is strong evidence that these are not the additions of followers but his actual claims.

It is not possible to eliminate these claims from the teaching of the carpenter of Nazareth. It cannot be said that they were invented by the evangelists, nor even that they were unconsciously exaggerated. They are widely and evenly distributed in the different Gospels and sources of the Gospels, and the portrait is too consistent and too balanced to have been imagined (John R. W. Stott, *Basic Christianity*).

Although we don't get into it here (see Tough Questions guide *How Reliable Is the Bible?*), there is ample evidence for the reliability of the gospel records, another reason to have confidence that the claims we read are virtually identical to Jesus' statements.

Question 9: **What are some of the implications for all humanity if Jesus really was the unique Son of God?**

Question 10: **What are some implications for your life if Jesus was God come to earth in human form? What is your emotional reaction to that idea?** Some people will be very comforted by the realization that Jesus clearly spelled out who he was, and that God loved them enough to send his Son. That very same reality will make others uncomfortable. Some may be angry because of the apparent narrowness of Jesus' claims. Be prepared for a range of reactions. Note: A good leader learns to be a good listener during these moments and patiently encourages members to feel comfortable sharing their honest answers.

Question 11: **What priority did Jesus place on accepting his true identity?** Our salvation is dependent upon knowing and affirming the true identity of Jesus. You cannot be saved from the penalty of sin without acknowledging your need for a Savior. You cannot enter the kingdom of God without acknowledging its King. You cannot be forgiven sin without a relationship with the One who forgave you.

Question 12: **What do you think is behind people's emotional reactions in thinking Jesus' claims are offensive? What is the hardest thing for you to accept about his claims?**

Question 13: **On a scale from one to ten, place an X near the spot and phrase [see guide] that best describes you. What reasons do you have for placing your X where you did?**

DISCUSSION TWO

How Is Jesus Different from Other Religious Leaders?

Short Answer: Though many other great religious leaders gave wisdom for living life, none made the radical claim to be God in the flesh and the only forgiver of sins—and none rose from the dead.

Question 1: **Describe a time when you observed or experienced bigotry or prejudice in action. What particularly angers you about such behavior?**

Question 2: Some people think commitment to one particular religious point of view is like bigotry—a sort of spiritual prejudice. Do you agree? Explain.

Question 3: What are some bad reasons for strong religious feelings? Describe someone you know who exhibits such unreasonable or irrational convictions. People often hold a religious opinion with a tenacity and smugness that exposes their underlying spiritual bigotry. Christians are not exempt from this fault. To say, "I have the truth because I'm smart and have figured it out, and you're wrong because you're not as enlightened as I am" is arrogance, even if you do believe the right things about Jesus. But when a Christian humbly admits that it is Jesus himself who compels us to affirm his uniqueness, that is not bigotry; it is simply handling the claims of Jesus with accuracy. Note: When members of your group describe people with unreasonable convictions, don't allow them to use actual names and don't permit ridicule.

Question 4: Read the following statements [see guide]. Put an *A* in front of those you agree with; put a *D* if you disagree.

Question 5: In the following chart [see guide], the only religion completely dependent on its founder is Christianity. Do you agree that this is the case? Explain.

Question 6: How different would Christianity be if Jesus had claimed only to be a prophet (like Muhammad or Elijah) instead of the Son of God?

Question 7: What is your explanation for Jesus' apparent narrow-mindedness [see guide]? Jesus could have been wrong, and his narrow-mindedness evidence of egotism or sincere self-delusion. But if Jesus was right, he wasn't narrow-minded. There's nothing narrow about the God of the universe saying, "I'm the God of the universe." That's a simple fact. What's narrow is someone saying, "I'm the only truth," when there are seemingly lots of other sources. Jesus is saying, "Whatever good any other person can do for you, no one can save you except me." Oswald Chambers observed, "We can get to God as Creator apart from Jesus Christ, but never to God as our Father except through him" (*Christian Discipline,* vol. 2). If that is really true, Jesus' words aren't limiting—they're a statement of warning, love, and safety.

Question 8: **Is it possible we misunderstood what Jesus meant? Explain why you think that.** The possibility of misunderstanding has to be granted, simply because we're finite humans, who can be mistaken. But Jesus explained himself in so many different ways and with so many different titles and examples, we can have certainty beyond a reasonable doubt that he really meant for us to treat him as utterly unlike any leader or prophet who has ever lived. Be sure to draw out why members of your group responded the way they have.

Question 9: **Why do you think people try to soften Jesus' stark claims and keep some aspects of his teaching without fully recognizing his deity? Why would that be dishonest and a distortion of Jesus' message?** Outright rejection of Jesus would not necessarily be popular, so many people want to remake Jesus so he fits into their life without making demands on them. Any time we put words into Jesus' mouth that he didn't say—or take away words he did—we set ourselves up as superior to him. Surely, one of the reasons Jesus said things in the radical way he did was so we would wrestle with his claims and come to the truth instead of easily writing him off and missing the point of his coming.

In an article called "Worshipping the Unknown God: The Heathen and Salvation," Greg Koukl notes, "This is why Jesus is so offensive. If you talk about God, everyone smiles and nods approval. Mention Jesus, though, and sparks fly. Jesus is God with a face, not the fill-in-the-blank variety we conform to our own tastes. He can't be twisted, distorted, and stuffed in our back pocket. That bothers people" (*Clear Thinking,* Fall 1995).

Question 10: What is your reaction to the above story [see guide]? With what parts can you identify? Do any parts trouble you? Which ones and why?

Question 11: As a result of this session, how would you sum up what makes Jesus different from all other religious leaders?

Question 12: On a scale from one to ten, place an X near the spot and phrase [see guide] that best describes you. What reasons do you have for placing your X where you did?

DISCUSSION THREE

Did Jesus Really Claim to Be God?

Short Answer: Though he humbly lived out his role as a servant, Jesus' teachings and actions made it clear he was both God and man.

Question 1: When you were growing up, what were you led to believe about Santa Claus? What was the effect on you when you found out he wasn't real?

Question 2: In your early years, what were you taught about who Jesus was? Mark your answer on the continuum below [see guide]. What reasons were supplied to persuade you that what you were learning was fact, not just dogma?

Question 3: Why do you think the biographers of Jesus recorded details about Jesus' simple, human qualities? For an accurate picture of Jesus to emerge, we must see his full humanity as well as his deity. Modern people are more inclined to doubt his divine role (or to doubt his existence altogether), but there were also some in the early church who doubted Jesus' humanity. That is why, as early as the writings of the apostle John, it was pointed out that "Jesus Christ has come in the flesh" (1 John 4:1–3). This confusion about Jesus blossomed into a full-blown heresy called "docetism" and in the second century, "gnosticism." These people taught that God would not—and could not— condescend to take on humanity, so Jesus had just "appeared" (the Greek word is *dokeo,* hence *docetism*) to be a man. Their Jesus was only a spirit, a phantom who had no human birth, left no footprints as he walked, and did not really suffer on the cross.

Christian Science is a group today that embodies a similarly mistaken view of Jesus. Christian Science teaches that the physical world is not real, and so Jesus did not have flesh, because there is no such thing. It teaches that "the Christ" is separate from the man Jesus. The main thing for your group members to wrestle with here is that, whatever else we say about Jesus, he was fully human, just like us.

Question 4: **Why do you think the biographers of Jesus included these details about his life [see guide]?** The apostle John explained that he knew many stories about Jesus, but his reason for writing was so "you may believe that Jesus is the Christ, the Son of God, and that by believing you may have life in his name" (John 20:31). The other gospel writers were also persuaded that Jesus was unlike any man who had ever lived. But rather than just claim that, they recorded the many unusual and miraculous things Jesus did, so for all time people could review the data for themselves and come to their own conclusions.

Question 5: **What would you conclude if your next-door neighbor made the above claims [see guide]? Explain.**

Question 6: **If Jesus didn't want us to think he was God, how could he have made that clear? Do you know of any incident in which Jesus apparently tried to deny his divinity?** Someone familiar with the Bible may point out that at his trial, Jesus seemed to deny the charge of blasphemy by telling his accusers, "Well, that's what you say (about me)" when they demanded he proclaim whether or not he was the Christ (Messiah), the Son of God. Some translations use the phrase "You have said it yourself" or "You say that I am." That may sound to our ears as if Jesus were denying the charge or at least evading the question.

The reality is that Jesus was answering clearly in the affirmative. First, the phrase is not evasive but an unequivocal statement of agreement. When Judas asked if he was the one who would betray Jesus, Jesus used the same phrase: "You have said it yourself" (Matthew 26:25 NASB). Was Jesus telling Judas he wasn't the betrayer? Second, the words following Jesus' answer at his trial make it unmistakably clear that he was claiming the role of Messiah. He quoted a passage from the book of Daniel, in which "the Son of Man"—another messianic title—judges the whole world at the end of time. In effect Jesus was saying, "Men, you may be my judges now, but a time is coming when you'll appear before me in my heavenly court!" (See Mark 14:61–62.) If Jesus had not been the Son of God, such a statement would have been blasphemous; it is the phrase that condemned him. It is one of the strongest claims to Jesus' divinity in the Bible, and it comes straight out of his mouth. (Note: This information need not be brought up unless a group member asks.)

Question 7: **Clearly, some people find the possibility that we are a "visited planet"—that God came and lived among us—very exciting and hopeful. Yet history shows a widespread hostility to this understanding of Jesus' life. Why might this idea sometimes spark angry opposition?**

Question 8: **What are the implications for your life if Jesus really was God in the flesh? What is a difficult or troublesome aspect of this truth for your life today?** To ignore Jesus or to relegate him to a low-priority status would be unthinkable if he is really God's messenger to earth. Our lives simply cannot remain the same when we know that the great Creator of the universe has come among us to tell us of his love and his desire to forgive us and become leader of our lives.

Yet many people do that very thing. They are like the man C. S. Lewis described who "is deliberately trying not to know whether Christianity is true or false, because he foresees endless trouble if it should turn out to be true. He is like the man who deliberately 'forgets' to look at the notice board because, if he did, he might find his name down for some unpleasant duty." Lewis continues, "You may not be certain yet whether you ought to be a Christian; but you do know you ought to be a man, not an ostrich, hiding its head in the sand" *(God in the Dock: Essays on Theology and Ethics)*.

Your group members may feel bad that they haven't made Jesus a priority or that their lives haven't lived up to his ideal. They may also be troubled by the narrowness of it all. One clear implication of God putting all of who he was in Jesus is that other truths, paths, and religions have more error in them than many have previously supposed. So although it's good news that we have a Savior in Jesus, it can trouble people to think about that ramification in regard to their imperfect lives and to the lives of others who don't even care about Jesus.

Question 9: Based on what you have discussed in this session, what would you say to someone who proposed that Jesus claimed to be only a teacher or rabbi?

Question 10: What do you think it would take (or what did it take) for you to come to the same conclusion as Thomas and say, as he finally did, "[Jesus, you are] my Lord and my God!" (John 20:28)? There is an intellectual side to this conclusion (the recognition of Jesus' deity) and an emotional side (the personal embracing of him). The first says, "Jesus, you are the Lord," and the second says, "Jesus, you are my Lord." Of course, Jesus is not content with convincing us of his identity; he wants us to welcome and accept him as the leader of our lives.

Question 11: On a scale from one to ten, place an *X* near the spot and phrase [see guide] that best describes you. What reasons do you have for placing your *X* where you did?

DISCUSSION FOUR

Why Focus on Jesus' Death?

Short Answer: Jesus' mission was not finished until he died a sacrificial death for sin; Christians emphasize his death because he himself did so—it was the culmination of everything he came to earth to do.

Question 1: Do you remember a time when you got into really big trouble when you were growing up? What were the consequences for you?

Question 2: How is forgiving someone's wrongdoing against you similar to forgiving a debt he or she owes you? In the spiritual realm, every sin rings up indebtedness—we take something away from God with each act of defiance. We exist not because of any action on our part but wholly because God, out of his great love, wanted to give us the experience of life. He owes us nothing; we owe him everything. And each of our sins takes away some of the glory he is due as our Creator.

Picture each sin as the refusal to make a mortgage payment. If we stop sinning (repent) and start giving God glory, that would be like starting to make mortgage payments after ceasing to do so. Yet we still owe for the times we didn't make the payments, even if we keep up with current amounts due. How will we make the past-due payments? The Bible tells us the debt is too great and life is not long enough to ever pay in full—we just don't have it in us to give God what is his due and to make up for our offenses. That is why Christ's death, as a payment for us, is so precious: it releases us from ever having to worry that our spiritual mortgage will lapse. Jesus paid it all—not only past due amounts but the balance as well. Spiritually speaking, there are no more payments due, ever. We are full owners of this thing called life, and the spiritual mansion we anticipate moving into, in heaven, is already ours because Christ paid the balance on the cross.

Question 3: Sin is often compared to a debt we owe God. In what sense would offending God (sinning) create a debt to him?

Question 4: Early in the Bible (Genesis 3:21), when the first humans commit the first sin, what does God do to show his care for them in spite of their rebellion against him? Although it was cruel and necessarily bloody, what teaching about the cost of sin might God be trying to communicate through this symbolism? Think of how differently we would view sin if every time we did something wrong, we were obligated to sacrifice a small animal to pay for that offense. Would we be as quick to go that route if we knew a death was the consequence? The irony is that every sin does create moral indebtedness with God—the pain of the animal is just a physical representation of that pain.

When God clothed Adam and Eve, he showed his care for them. Clothing them with animal skins foreshadowed what price would be necessary to make provision for their wrongdoing. It is interesting to note that when Adam wanted to make his own covering, he used fig leaves. Yet God's initiative required animal hides. This parallels human-made religion and God-ordained religion. Throughout the ages, people have tried to solve their spiritual problem by using their own means—with results as humorous and ineffective as Adam's. God's means are more costly but effective. And Christ's sacrifice was the most costly, and most effective, of all.

Question 5: **What were the ancient Israelites instructed to do in Exodus 12:21–27? What lesson would the people learn about the relationship between a covering of blood and death's power?** The people of Israel would understand in the most powerful way that a covering of blood protected them from death. In the same way, the covering of Christ's blood shields us completely from eternal death. Note: Remember that some members of the group may not have Bibles with them, so be sure to earmark the passage to be read in your own Bible before the meeting.

Question 6: **What did God want the Israelites to do as a solution to the problem (Numbers 21:7–9)? What lesson might this bizarre episode have taught the people about the need for faith in God and about the futility of self-effort to gain God's approval?**

Question 7: Jesus referred to the above story [see guide] and compared it to his own crucifixion (John 3:14–16; 12:32–33). What parallels do you see between these two events and how the benefits provided by God are received? The people of Israel could do nothing except look at the serpent up on the pole and believe. There were no elaborate rituals, no self-help programs, no action on their part other than to respond in faith and trust God to do for them what they were unable to do for themselves.

Jesus was like that serpent, lifted up on a cross for all to see (John 3:14–15). We are all dying with the venom of sin. We can do nothing to save ourselves from its deadly poison; we must simply accept, on faith, that God can save us. It is not that there are lots of remedies and this is the best one—there simply is no other cure.

Question 8: What is the purpose in paying a kidnapper a ransom? Jesus said his life would be given "as a ransom for many" (Matthew 20:28). Why would Jesus say we need to be ransomed—in what sense has the human race been kidnapped and held captive? Satan is the original kidnapper of the human race. Because he prevailed when he tempted Adam and Eve, they—and the rest of us—belong to him (1 John 5:19; Matthew 4:8–9; John 14:30; Ephesians 6:11–12). One purpose of Jesus' death was to buy us back from the dominion of the evil one.

Question 9: John the Baptist called Jesus "the Lamb of God, who takes away the sin of the world" (John 1:29). How is Jesus like the Passover lamb you read about earlier?

Question 10: Some people find it offensive to place emphasis on sacrifices and innocent animals dying. What is your reaction to these historical events and commands from God?

Question 11: What is your reaction to Jesus' mission of giving up his life on your behalf? Why would any story about the purpose of Jesus' life and death be woefully incomplete without this crucial point? A crossless Christianity is promise without fulfillment. It is hope for salvation from sin, with no basis. It is God coming among us but not willing to suffer for us. It is words without power. It is children who've been talked to for their wrongdoing but not forgiven. It is a prophet but no deliverer. In a crossless Christianity, we are all still in our sins, looking eye-to-eye at the One we sinned against, without any certainty of absolution.

Question 12: On a scale from one to ten, place an *X* near the spot and phrase [see guide] that best describes you. What reasons do you have for placing your *X* where you did?

DISCUSSION FIVE

Isn't the Resurrection of Jesus a Myth?

Short Answer: No, it's a well-attested fact of history and foundational to the truth of Christianity.

General note: Some critics of the Resurrection have rightly observed that other religions have an idea of a rising god. Various fertility cults have a god that comes back to life each spring. The Egyptian god Osiris, husband of Isis, also "resurrected." (Isis also had a son, Horus, who was "miraculously" conceived without a living father—claimed as yet another parallel to Christianity.) In the secular realm, Thomas Paine observed, "The story of Jesus Christ appearing after he was dead is the story of an apparition. . . . Stories of this kind had been told of the assassination of Julius Caesar." Because of these parallels, the uniqueness of Jesus' resurrection becomes suspect—as does the event itself.

Despite parallels, there are vast differences between Jesus' resurrection and these myths or legends. The fertility gods resurrect annually; Jesus' resurrection was once and for all. Hearsay stories of other resurrections did not create a group of followers willing to die for those claims, but Jesus' disciples were prepared to do so—and all but one did. Besides, Jesus' followers were Jewish, and Jesus' resurrection blew apart their religious convention. The greatly renowned German New Testament scholar Joachim Jeremias states, "Nowhere does one find in the [Jewish] literature anything comparable to the resurrection of Jesus. Certainly resurrections of the dead were known, but these always concerned resuscitations, the return to the earthly life. In no place in the late Judaic literature does it concern a resurrection to doxa (glory) as an event of history" (quoted by William Craig, "Contemporary Scholarship and the Historical Evidence for the Resurrection of Jesus Christ").

The rebirth idea prevalent among various cultures may even be "hardwired" in the human soul, put there by God so we would recognize Jesus (just as a conscience and God awareness seem hardwired into every person, regardless of culture). So if the objection is raised that other religions have a rising god and therefore Jesus' resurrection is not unique, be ready to make your contribution to the discussion by pointing out that Jesus' resurrection is both categorically different and historically substantiated.

Question 1: Describe a situation in which you were asked to trust someone who turned out not to be trustworthy. How did you feel about what happened?

Question 2: Describe a time when you were sure things were going to turn out terribly, but somehow the outcome was better than you anticipated. What did that happy ending do to you?

Question 3: What does Matthew 16:21 indicate was the disciples' area of misunderstanding?

Question 4: What do you think of this theory [see guide]?

Question 5: What do you think of the above theory [see guide]? Does the evidence point to hopeful disciples, intent on seeing their leader again as he promised they would? Or does the record show a discouraged band of disbelievers?

Question 6: What do you think of this theory [see guide]?

Question 7: **Which of the following points gives you the best reason(s) for dismissing this theory [see guide]? Why does that particular point make sense to you?**

Question 8: **Which of the above arguments [see guide] seems strong to you? Explain.**

Question 9: **Why do you think Jesus' resurrection is such an emotionally charged issue?** A dead man rising is not your everyday occurrence, and it stretches the limits of what a rational person can accept. Actually, this is one of the reasons why God did it—so it would be spectacular beyond comparison and would prove itself to be the all-time most dramatic miracle. As such, it's a beacon, a signal that something was going on in Jesus' life that was totally unlike anything in history.

Question 10: **What is hard for you to accept when it comes to the subject of Jesus' resurrection?** Group members may come up with a number of problems with the Resurrection, but each probably stems from the highly unusual and statistically unlikely occurrence of a dead man coming back to life.

In spite of rational difficulties with the Resurrection, if we grant that God is Creator, then it really isn't such a stretch to imagine that the Giver of life and Creator of the cosmos can remake a dead corpse into a living being again. He who made the first man out of nonliving dirt can just as easily make the "last Adam," Jesus (1 Corinthians 15:45), out of the remains left in the tomb. In the same way, God will remake all believers, regardless of the state of decay, into resurrected people to live with him forever (Philippians 3:20–21).

Question 11: **What additional evidence would help you gain more certainty about the Resurrection?** These points by Edwin M. Yamauchi might be helpful additional evidence:

> Not even the most skeptical can deny the historical attestation of the faith of the early Christians in the resurrection

of Christ. This simple fact is of importance if we accept as genuine the numerous predictions of Jesus concerning his death and resurrection (Matthew 16:21; 17:9, 22, 23; 20:18, 19; 26:2; etc.). Charlatans such as Theudas (Josephus, Antiquities XX. 5.1), who claimed to have the power to divide the Jordan River, or the Gnostic Menander, who claimed his disciples would remain ageless, were quickly exposed by the failure of their claims. The Qumran community, which has some features in common with the Christian community, did not survive the destruction of its monastery by the Romans in A.D. 68 because the people had no comparable faith to sustain them.

—"Easter: Myth, Hallucination, or History?"

Perhaps William Lane Craig summarizes this subject best when he writes,

None of the previous counter-explanations can account for the evidence as plausibly as the resurrection itself. One might ask, "Well, then, how do skeptical scholars explain the facts of the resurrection appearances, the empty tomb, and the origin of the Christian faith?" The fact of the matter is, they don't. Modern scholarship recognizes no plausible explanatory alternative to the resurrection of Jesus. Those who refuse to accept the resurrection as a fact of history are simply self-confessedly left without an explanation.

These three great facts—the resurrection appearances, the empty tomb, and the origin of the Christian faith—all point unavoidably to one conclusion: The resurrection of Jesus. Today the rational man can hardly be blamed if he believes that on that first Easter morning a divine miracle occurred.

—"Contemporary Scholarship and the Historical Evidence for the Resurrection of Jesus Christ"

Question 12: **On a scale from one to ten, place an X near the spot and phrase [see guide] that best describes you. What reasons do you have for placing your X where you did?**

What Impact Does Jesus Make Today?

Short Answer: Jesus' influence is in direct proportion to the access we grant him into our lives and souls.

Question 1: **What are some ways you've observed people going astray in the name of following Jesus? Do you think that was Jesus' fault? Explain.** It is almost always a fundamental misunderstanding about Jesus that causes people to do wrong things in his name. The problem isn't Jesus; it's the failure of his followers to truly follow him consistently.

Question 2: **What are some of the good things you believe Jesus has brought to the world (even if you are not personally a believer in him)?**

Question 3: **How would your life be different if there were no Christian influence in the world?** Even if people don't follow Jesus, they are the beneficiaries of those in society who do (as noted in the Straight Talk "Imagine," just before this question).

Question 4: **Based on the following passages [see guide], how would Jesus answer these questions?** Here is one way to put Jesus' answers to life's biggest questions:

- *Is there a God?* Yes, and he wants to have first place in the hearts of his creatures.
- *Why am I here?* To live life to the full by being in a love relationship with God, first and foremost, and by loving your fellow creatures as well.
- *Where am I ultimately going?* God's desire is to share heaven with you forever.

Question 5: **How would you describe Jesus' version of life's priorities, based on the following passages [see guide]?** A life with Jesus boils down to loving others, not using them. It also calls us to put his kingdom first and to live by faith instead of frantically trying to accumulate the "stuff" of life and missing its real purpose.

Question 6: Based on the passages below [see guide], how does Jesus offer help through life's hard times?

Question 7: Considering the passages below [see guide], what does Jesus promise to those who place their trust in him?

Question 8: What aspects of Jesus' teaching seem to you to be too good to be true?

Question 9: What do you think would characterize the life of someone thoroughly convinced that the things Jesus said are true and that his promises are completely trustworthy? Your group members will come up with a variety of answers here, but based on the passages cited in question 7, a fundamental difference most certainly would be a sense of peace. Life's circumstances would cease to be the indicators—or producers—of life's greatest happiness; rather connection with God and conformity to his will would be paramount.

Question 10: What holds you back from completely accepting Jesus' provision of forgiveness and leadership of your life? Pay special attention to the responses you hear from the members of your group, as their answers could provide a great opportunity for you to engage in further conversation on an individual basis regarding their level of openness or readiness to becoming a Christian.

Question 11: What is one step you could take right now to give yourself (or more of yourself) to Jesus as best you know how, with whatever faith you have? Be sensitive to the possibility that this question could lead to a significant spiritual decision at this juncture. You may have a seeker in your group tell you he or she is ready at this point to receive Christ, or a lapsed believer may indicate readiness to "come home." Treat the moment reverently.

Question 12: On a scale from one to ten, place an X near the spot and phrase [see guide] that best describes you. What reasons do you have for placing your X where you did?

CHAPTER THREE

How Reliable Is the Bible?

DISCUSSION ONE

Where Did the Bible Come From?

Short Answer: The Bible was written by many people over many centuries.

Question 1: What do you remember hearing or believing about the Bible as you were growing up? Were you an "easy sell" or did you tend to be skeptical about its contents?

Question 2: What nagging doubts about the Bible do you have now? If the sessions in this guide could answer one question for you, what would that be?

Question 3: Do you think there's any value in having more than just "dictated pronouncements from God" in the Bible? Explain. When the biblical writers include details about themselves or others, how does this enhance what God supposedly said and did in their lives?

Question 4: **What might be the disadvantages of having so many authors put together a book? How might this process add value to the end result?** Having the background and experience of people in the Bible helps make it a fully human book. It gives us the context so we can better understand its message. It tells us what humans thought and felt, which aids in our sense of connection with them and helps us relate to their clearly human actions and reactions. That there is variety and yet consistency in spite of having many different authors gives the Bible's claim of divine inspiration greater credibility.

Question 5: What kind of validation would need to be provided by someone who claims to be giving us ultimate truth?

Question 6: What safeguards are inherent in a centuries-long process of confirming the books of the Bible? Such a lengthy confirmation process would safeguard the Bible against one person dominating the choices of which books to include, or a faction imposing their theological bias. God's people, over time, recognized (and that's an important word; it wasn't a vote per se, because the church can't make a work inspired) those books that came with divine authority and origin.

Question 7: If someone came today and said they had a book of truth that should be included in the Bible, what criteria would you use for evaluating their claim? When Christians centuries ago evaluated the books they received, they used a threefold test:

1. Did the book come from a prophet or apostle?
2. Did the book have doctrinal integrity—did it match revelation already accepted?
3. Did the book have wide acceptance—did many of God's people in several places validate these writings?

Such tests would probably preclude current books because

- the claim to prophetic status or apostolic authority could probably not be substantiated. (Joseph Smith, the Mormon prophet, fails the qualifications of a prophet because he gave some false predictions and taught things contrary to God's Word.)
- the book would probably be at variance with some teaching in the Bible. (Books like the Book of Mormon or Science and Health, which claim to be from God, contradict biblical teaching.)
- any contender today would have to be circulated among Christians all over the world in every culture and be received by all, which is not very likely.

Question 8: Even if a modern-day psychic had a ninety percent accuracy rate, would he or she pass the first test above? How would this test rate a prophet like Joseph Smith of the Latter-day Saints (Mormons), who made several prophecies that never came true—even though he made some which did? Because biblical prophets must be one hundred percent accurate, virtually all of today's so-called prophetic activity would be deemed spurious. In Old Testament days, prophets weren't likely to make such rash or careless predictions as those we see today, because death was the punishment for any incorrect statement following "Thus says the Lord." While capital punishment for false prophets is not appropriate in our day and age, rejection of the message and the messenger is a timeless biblical principle, and we would do well to follow it.

Question 9: What would the second test, of theological accuracy, do to many who claim prophetic messages today and even appear to have miraculous powers, yet teach unbiblical theology? Most people today are impressed by an unusual prediction, regardless of what else the person says. But some messages should be rejected no matter how "miraculous" the source (see Galatians 1:8). The Bible is clear that something unusual may not originate from God, and bad theology certainly doesn't. We need to be less impressed by what appears to be supernatural, and more discerning about the source—and what tags along with a message. To use a fishing analogy, we should be wary of swallowing a dangerous theological or pseudo-spiritual "hook" when we bite the "worm" of a supposedly miraculous event or prediction.

Question 10: What is troublesome to you about believing that the Bible is the sole written authority from God and that it is superior to all other religious books?

Question 11: What would it take for you to place complete confidence in the Bible as truth from God and as the supreme written guide for your life?

Question 12: Pick the statement(s) [see guide] that best summarizes your view. What reasons do you have for your choice?

DISCUSSION TWO

Isn't the Bible Full of Myths?

Short Answer: No, not in the sense of stories that claim to be authentic but are fictional. The Bible contains many made-up stories, but those are clearly identified as such.

Question 1: What is a tall tale or myth you've heard that is popular but not based on history? Why do people enjoy telling these less than truthful stories?

Question 2: What is something in the Bible you think is a myth (or is commonly believed to be a myth)? What aspects of that story seem unreal?

Question 3: When people speak of the Bible as being full of myths, to which of the above types [see guide] are they referring? What do you think might have motivated a biblical writer who allegedly penned such a myth? Many allege that the Bible contains all three kinds of myths mentioned in the Straight Talk preceding this question. The most scandalous myths, however, are those in which religious dogma is put forth as real and necessary to believe, but for which there is little historical or rational support. Those who contend that the Bible includes this type of myth would describe that part of the Bible as sort of a "pious fraud," where a writer thought something would help others even if he knew it wasn't true. Also, people might say the storyteller thought the material was something God wanted him to write, so he went ahead, hoping for some divine reward, even though he knew he was making it up. Another possible motive for fraud is the writer's hope for power or prestige that would follow publication.

Question 4: What clues would you look for in trying to determine if a story in the Bible was meant to be taken at face value? Most stories in the Bible that are parables or fiction are introduced with verbal clues as to their nature. Examples include such statements as "Suppose a man had two sons ..." and "I will tell you what heaven is like...." Historical material, on the other hand, omits such disclaimers and has lots of detail typical of eyewitness accounts.

Question 5: **Do you think believers generally investigate the biblical stories they read to determine whether they have a basis in fact? Why do you think some people are so ready to accept everything they read in the Bible without questioning it?** People may just be gullible by nature, and so they accept the Bible—a good thing—for bad reasons. If these people had been in another culture, they may have accepted the wrong things with the same uncritical approval. God doesn't commend gullibility. If you or your group members' foundation for truth is shaky, it's never too late to get good reasons for good beliefs.

Question 6: **Do you believe that critics of the Bible's miraculous stories have solid evidence that contradicts the Bible's claims? What other possible motives or reasons might lay behind a skeptical stance?** Most critics are surprisingly emotional when it comes to their criticism of the Bible's miraculous elements. We who believe would do well to listen better as we relate to these people. It can help immensely to learn how such a critical attitude developed. Most likely, the person was forced to accept things without question at an early age and was never encouraged to test the reliability or reasonableness of the belief system presented to them. That can leave a bitter taste in a person's mouth when it comes to spiritual truth. You may want to use this question to address some of your group members' issues regarding their skeptical stance toward the Bible.

Question 7: **How does the presence of other flood stories affect the probability of a historical event giving rise to them all?** If a worldwide event such as the flood in Noah's time truly happened, one would expect that there would be many stories concerning that event in various cultures. "The Flood is told of by the Greeks, the Hindus, the Chinese, the Mexicans, the Algonquins, and the Hawaiians. Also, one list of Sumerian kings treats the Flood as a real event" (Norman Geisler and Ron Brooks, *When Skeptics Ask*). The presence of numerous accounts distributed among many peoples increases the historical probability that the event described actually occurred, even if the accounts vary somewhat.

Question 8: Do you think it is reasonable to accept the historical accuracy of the more difficult parts of the Bible when the witness of Jesus and other verifiable claims show its overall trustworthiness? Why or why not?

Question 9: Why is it sometimes hard to accept stories that contain supernatural elements?

Question 10: What kind of research could a person do to help him or her gain more confidence in the stories told in the Bible? Books on archaeology and comparative studies in other literature similar to the Bible would be a great place to start reading. Another thing to do might be to talk to others who trust the Bible and find out why they believe in it.

Question 11: On a scale from one to ten, place an *X* near the spot and phrase [see guide] that best describes you. What reasons do you have for placing your *X* where you did?

DISCUSSION THREE

What About All Those Contradictions?

Short Answer: The claim of contradictions in the Bible is grossly exaggerated, and the problems that do exist can be harmonized.

Question 1: Can you recall a time when you saw or heard something disturbing about someone you trusted? What was it like to feel mistrust for someone who had been worthy of trust up to that point?

Question 2: Have you read anything in the Bible that you believe is a true contradiction? Explain. What has this done to your level of confidence in the Bible?

Question 3: Do you think this issue of how God is portrayed [see guide] constitutes a contradiction? Why or why not?

Question 4: To what extent does your view of God incorporate the different aspects (listed above) of who God is [see guide]? How might your view of him need to be revised? These questions (and the information in the accompanying Straight Talk "Contradictions and the Character of God") form a sort of test case for how to resolve an alleged contradiction in the Bible. Sometimes it's as easy as just making the effort to understand the context, point of view, or intent of the different writers. At the same time, we have to be open to new ways of understanding familiar concepts. (In the example, we need to broaden our concept of God, not accuse the writers of contradicting each other.) When we do this, we can see that the Bible is in harmony with itself.

Question 5: Do you think these inscriptions [see guide] constitute a contradiction? Why or why not?

Question 6: What additional light is added by the detail from John 19:20, which states, "Many of the Jews read this sign, for the place where Jesus was crucified was near the city, and the sign was written in Aramaic, Latin and Greek"? If one of the cross inscriptions read, "Rudolph the Red-Nosed Reindeer," then we'd have a contradiction! The variations shown in the Straight Talk "Contradictions and the Cross" reveal partial information recorded in each gospel, but not contradictory information. Also, that there were three inscriptions in different languages could account for some of the variations; if the inscriptions were slightly different in the different languages, one gospel writer could have recorded only what one language said, and other writers could have recorded the other, slightly differently worded inscription.

Question 7: Does the slight variation in this wording offer any positive evidence that the gospel writers are reliable historians? Explain. What do the differences in wording suggest about the integrity of the early copyists who let the differences remain in the manuscripts? By leaving the apparent contradictions, the copyists show there was no attempt to collude or artificially correct the text. They believed it was better to be accurate and preserve manuscript integrity than to harmonize.

Question 8: **If God is behind the Bible, why do you think he hasn't eliminated all possible areas of confusion?** Human beings are prone to misunderstanding, simply because we are finite. Nothing is beyond potential confusion as long as we're human. That doesn't mean we can't have substantial understanding, but it does mean that there's nothing God could do, short of granting us omniscience, to eliminate all possible error in our thinking.

Take, for example, the simple sign "No Parking After Two-Inch Snowfall." Patrick C. Heston, in his tongue-in-cheek article "Theology of a City Street Sign" *(The Wittenburg Door),* points out the many ways this sign could be understood—or misunderstood:

- Is it a command ("don't do it") or a description ("try as you may, you won't be able to")?
- Is it literal snow or could it allude to figurative elements including cocaine or heroin?
- The sign doesn't say where the snow must fall—what if it's in the next county?
- Does the snow have to fall all at once, or could two or three snowfalls accumulate past two inches?
- What if some of the snow fell before midnight, and the rest after?
- What if it's a 1.9-inch snowfall?
- What if it snows more than two inches—is it limited to snowfalls of exactly two inches, no more, no less?
- What if it snows two inches but doesn't stick?
- Does it mean the first snowfall of two inches after the sign goes up, or every one after that?
- Does it mean cars only or include trucks? What about boats?
- Does the sign prohibit parking everywhere in the city after snow or just the streets?

- If you've already parked before the snow falls, can you stay parked, because technically, you're not parking after the two-inch snowfall?
- Does it mean "after" in the sense of "in the manner of"—so you can't park the way snow falls?
- How soon after the snow falls can you park again?

Clearly, any simple statement can be disputed—all the more a statement that is complicated or abstract. That's why we need to follow good principles of interpretation. The amazing thing about the Bible is how much is agreed upon in spite of the many ways its message could be understood.

Question 9: Other than a desire to seek truth, what might motivate someone to look for contradictions in the Bible? What does it tell you about a person when he or she seems to delight in trying to ridicule the Bible?

Question 10: How might the above rules [see guide] help you to handle problems that arise when you're reading the Bible?

Question 11: Pick the statement(s) [see guide] that best summarizes your view. What reasons do you have for your choice?

DISCUSSION FOUR

Hasn't the Bible Changed Over Time?

Short Answer: No, the ancient manuscripts we now have assure us that current translations are extremely close to the original text.

Question 1: Do you remember a funny story about a time when you gave someone important instructions and they misunderstood you (or vice versa)? Describe what happened.

Question 2: Does knowing that the Bible has been translated so many times cause you to lose confidence in the accuracy of the Bible you read now? Why or why not?

Question 3: **Do you think it's a problem that no original of any book of the Bible exists from which to make translations? Why or why not?** Because the copies we have are dated so early, although the originals are lost, there is certainty about virtually 99.9 percent of the Bible. And no questionable verse is the basis for any doctrine.

Question 4: **In view of the above table [see guide], what is your reaction to the number of New Testament manuscripts in comparison with the number of other works of ancient history?**

Question 5: **What do you think is the value of having all these citations from the New Testament in nonbiblical sources [see guide]?** The wide distribution of biblical texts is a safeguard against corruption because there are so many manuscripts to compare. Nothing in all of ancient literature even comes close to the massive amount of manuscript evidence for the New Testament.

Question 6: **How do these rules for accurate transmission [see guide] affect your overall trust in the text of the Bible?**

Question 7: **Does nonbiblical support for biblical events make any difference to you when you read the Bible? Why or why not?**

Question 8: **What bearing do these kinds of archaeological discoveries have on your trust in the Bible?** Knowing that nonbiblical sources and archaeological discoveries support various details about biblical history helps us see with even more certainty that the Bible writers were concerned with accurate history, not just with writing a biased "sales brochure" for Christianity.

Another great example of archaeological confirmation is the prophecy in Ezekiel about the city of Tyre. After thirteen years under seige, in 572 B.C. the city of Tyre made terms with the most powerful army in the world, the Babylonians. The city's name meant "rock," and after holding out against Nebuchadnezzar, it retained its island stronghold, though the mainland part of the city was destroyed.

Despite its reputation as an impregnable fortress ("the Rock"), the Bible predicted the future destruction of Tyre: "They will break down your walls and demolish your fine houses and throw your stones, timber and rubble into the sea" (Ezekiel 26:12, dated around 570 B.C. by most scholars). Adding to the odds against this prediction: most Middle East cities, once destroyed, were rebuilt on the same site after the ruins were covered with soil. Despite these facts, this prophecy was literally fulfilled in 332 B.C. by Alexander the Great. After demolishing the city, he cast all the debris (right down to the bare rock—especially ironic in light of the meaning of the word *Tyre*) into the sea to create a giant land bridge out to the island stronghold. This bridge still exists today and contains the ruins of Tyre—exactly as predicted.

Question 9: **What is the cumulative effect for you of all this evidence for the reliability of the Bible?**

Question 10: **Do you think if someone was intent on being skeptical, any amount of evidence would persuade? Do you think any error would convince someone committed to believing the Bible that there are reasons not to trust it? Explain your answers.** Of course, someone who just doesn't want to believe can't be convinced to do so. "No one will believe unless they are willing to believe" (Peter Kreeft and Ronald K. Tacelli, *Handbook of Christian Apologetics*). The only way to help such a person is to find out the real reason behind their resistance. Until that is identified, talking about other evidence is a waste of time. The discussion questions in this guide are designed to assist you in helping your group members uncover real reasons for their own resistance, past or present. Even in Jesus' day, people saw him perform miracles but didn't believe in him. For some, their hardness of heart kept them from belief, despite their recognition that he was extraordinary.

Question 11: **On a scale from one to ten, place an X near the spot and phrase [see guide] that best describes you. What reasons do you have for placing your X where you did?**

Why Should I Trust the Bible?

Short Answer: The Bible can be trusted because it is accurate, it bears evidence of divine authorship, and it was endorsed by Jesus, the most trustworthy person in history.

Question 1: What "heirloom story" have you heard about something a member of your family did in generations past? Do you consider this story truthful even though you weren't there? Why or why not?

Question 2: How does knowing that Jesus never wrote down a word of his teaching affect you as you read the Gospels? If you have confidence in what you're reading, what is the basis for that trust? Some people think that if Jesus had written his own book, we could have a more complete picture. Yet that is not necessarily the case. Autobiographies are not inherently more comprehensive or accurate—possibly, quite the contrary. Four writers rather than just one give us a fuller perspective, guarding against bias or failure to include the most relevant details.

Question 3: Why is it important to know that writers like Luke did research and that their historical statements stand up to later authentication? Most people are surprised to see statements like the first few verses in Luke's gospel, because the popular assumption is that history doesn't matter in the realm of religion. Yet Christianity is one of the few religions not based on a philosophy but rooted in historical events. If these events did not occur, whatever else it teaches is of little or no value.

Question 4: The assumption has been made that without modern methods of writing and copying, we can't know with any degree of certainty what Jesus actually said. Comment on this assumption in light of the following facts [see guide].

Question 5: The writers below [see guide] express that they were eyewitnesses of the events they recorded. Why is this important in documents meant to bring readers to faith?

Clearly, Peter, John, and Paul knew the difference between true events and "cleverly invented stories." They were giving their lives for things they saw and events they lived through. They knew that mixing in falsehood or exaggerations would damage their credibility. Considering the amount of persecution they endured, it was no small thing to be sure that what they were teaching was real.

Question 6: **Some people argue that because the gospel writers were followers of Jesus, they were biased and distorted historical information to agree with their bias. What is your reaction to this argument?**

Question 7: **From the above quotes [see guide], are you inclined to agree more with the reasoning of Carl Sagan or Wilbur Smith? Why?**

Question 8: **Other than supernatural involvement, what do you think could explain Jesus' fulfillment of messianic prophecies from the Bible?**

Question 9: **Many people will testify to the life-changing message they encounter in the Bible. What are both the strengths and weaknesses of this way of validating the trustworthiness of the Bible?** A myth can have a powerful effect on a person, as can a deliberate lie. The "change factor" of the Bible has limits with respect to how much it establishes the Bible's credibility. Muslims would say the Koran has changed their lives; does that mean it has to be God's Word? However, once a person sees that the Bible has credibility on other levels, it's good to know that not only is it right, it also works.

Question 10: **Between the last session and this one, what piece of evidence about the trustworthiness of the Bible has been most helpful to you?**

Question 11: **What aspects of the Bible's message are you more willing to consider since this study began?**

Question 12: **On a scale from one to ten, place an X near the spot and phrase [see guide] that best describes you.**

What reasons do you have for placing your *X* where you did?

DISCUSSION SIX

Is the Bible Really God's Book?

Short Answer: More than any other book in the world, the Bible has the stamp of divine involvement.

Question 1: From what you've observed, what unhealthy attitudes and practices can be adopted by people who believe that the Bible is God's Word? What positive changes have you seen?

Question 2: What evidence would someone need in order to gain confidence that any writings (including the Koran, the Book of Mormon, Science and Health, or other so-called revelations from God) are not just extraordinary but God's words? What comes from God must not just be true but also have power. Obviously, those writings must claim to be from God. The Bible is reliable, both historically and in terms of how its principles make a difference. As former president Calvin Coolidge said, "In this Book [the Bible] will be found the solution of all the problems of the world" (cited in *The Complete Book of Practical Proverbs and Wacky Wit* by Vern McLellan).

Question 3: Was there ever a time when you decided to find out once and for all if any writings (which may or may not have included the Bible) were really from God? If so, what did you discover in your search? If not, what would it take for you to embark on such an investigation?

Question 4: One piece of evidence people give in support of the Bible being divinely inspired is fulfilled prophecy. Do you believe this is sufficient to establish the Bible as God's book? Why or why not? One might argue that psychics sometimes predict things that eventually come true. Does that mean they are from God? There are vast differences between Bible prophecy and so-called psychics. For one,

Bible predictions came true centuries later. For another, Bible prophecies were very specific, unlike vague predictions such as, "Good fortune is coming your way." Finally, the Bible writers exalt God with accurate teaching about him, whereas psychics tend to exalt themselves and make money off the gullible public.

Question 5: Another reason people give as proof that the Bible is from God is the beneficial effects it has for those who believe its message. What are the strengths and weaknesses of such an argument?

Question 6: Which of the above premises [see guide] are strongest and which are weak, in your opinion? We think the strongest argument for the Bible's divine inspiration is the unconditional support it got from Jesus when he was here. Geisler and Brooks include the following chart in their book *When Skeptics Ask:*

What Jesus Taught About the Old Testament

1. Spirit-breathed—Matthew 22:43
2. Reliability—Matthew 26:54
3. Finality—Matthew 4:4, 7, 10
4. Sufficiency—Luke 16:31
5. Indestructibility—Matthew 5:17–18
6. Unity—Luke 24:27, 44
7. Clarity—Luke 24:27
8. Historicity—Matthew 12:40
9. Facticity (scientifically)—Matthew 19:2–5
10. Inerrancy—Matthew 22:29; John 5:39–40, 46–47
11. Infallibility—John 10:35

Anyone holding to an inferior position about Scripture must, in effect, contend with Jesus—not theologians—on this matter.

Question 7: Does the argument [see guide] convince you? Why or why not?

Question 8: **What other reasons have you heard or would you give for asserting that the Bible is God's Word?**

Question 9: **Do you believe it is enough to "just pray about it" to know if the Bible is from God? Why or why not?** Prayer is powerful, but prayer doesn't tell you if the Bible is God's Word. (Presumably, it's the answer to that prayer that would do that!) The Bible doesn't ever tell a person to use an answer to prayer as a way to sort out truth and error; we are all too prone to subjective influences to make this our final authority. As noted in the introduction to *How Reliable Is the Bible?* (see pp. 17–18), such methodology wouldn't help you distinguish between the Bible and other contenders with certainty sufficient to base your life on. We need hard data along with more subjective input.

Question 10: **What factors other than lack of evidence might contribute to your (or someone else's) hesitancy in accepting the Bible? What factors other than rational arguments might contribute to your (or someone else's) acceptance of the Bible?** The implications of the Bible's message have scared many people away from accepting it. Like Mark Twain, they see what it's demanding and they don't want to give in to those demands. They see that they will need to give an account to the God of the universe, and that may scare them.

As far as acceptance, sometimes people just read the Bible and like it, and for that simple reason they come to trust it. That's not bad, but it may not be enough to withstand future times of testing. Therefore, for those who come to belief easily, it's probably a good idea to fortify that foundation with more research into why the Bible is worth trusting.

Question 11: **What difference would it make in your everyday experience to believe that the Bible is God's Word?**

Question 12: **Pick the statement(s) [see guide] that best summarizes your view. What reasons do you have for your choice?**

CHAPTER FOUR

How Could God Allow Suffering and Evil?

DISCUSSION ONE

Where Did Evil Come From?

Short Answer: God did not *create* evil, but God did *allow* evil to enter the world as the consequence for sin after humankind's rebellion against God.

Question 1: **Describe a recent encounter you've had with some form of evil, which prompted you to wonder why this kind of thing ever happens.** This question is designed to be an icebreaker for your group as they discuss various encounters with hardship. People may have different definitions of the word *evil,* but don't let that distract your group from talking about situations that have caused them to wonder why bad things happen. After sharing openly about some of the difficulties faced in their lives, your group members will be better prepared to discuss this topic.

Question 2: **Who or what did you blame for the wrong that occurred in the situation you described above? Give reasons for your response. How did those around you see the situation?** An interesting side note is given by Peter Kreeft and Ronald K. Tacelli in their book *Handbook of Christian Apologetics:* "The fact that we do not naturally accept this world full of injustice, suffering, sin, disease and death—the very fact of our outrage at evil is a clue that we are in touch with a standard of goodness by which we judge this world as defective, as falling drastically short of the mark. The fact that we judge something evil might even be developed into an argument for the existence of the standard of Perfect Goodness implied in our judgment, and thus for the existence of the God of perfect goodness whom evil's existence seems to disprove."

Question 3: **Using your previous example, would you categorize that evil you experienced as moral evil, natural evil, or a combination of the two? Why? Does the category or type of evil influence how you determine where to place the blame for evil?** Most people feel that moral evil is the direct result of bad choices made by other humans, and that natural evil is something from God. Therefore they tend to blame people for moral evil, and God for natural evil. (Actually, they often blame God for not *preventing* moral evil, so he gets blame either way!) The reality is that both kinds of evil have their source in people, because natural evil wouldn't have ever happened if humankind hadn't sinned. Thus the more accurate picture is that humankind is responsible for both moral and natural evil, though group members need not arrive at that conclusion this early in the session.

Question 4: **Take your best shot at briefly explaining why we live in a world filled with so much evil and suffering.**

Question 5: **Summarized below are two conclusions based on the above observations [see guide]. Defend or refute the logic behind each.** This question invites group members to express their frustrations with how much evil there is in the world and allows them to wrestle with the argument that God may not even exist at all—or at least not in the form the Bible claims. Do not feel pressured to refute these points of view now, since alternative conclusions regarding the problem of evil are presented next.

Question 6: **The above explanation [see guide] introduces the element of a free choice by humankind to reject or accept God—with resulting consequences. Given the magnitude of the risk, what value do you suppose God placed on granting people freedom of choice (according to this perspective)?** Because God knew there was a risk that people would use their freedom to reject him (and as a result bring evil into the world), we can infer that God places a high value on freedom of choice. (Creating us in his image was a very important priority to God.) Given the extent of evil in our world, he must think freedom of choice is *extremely* valuable indeed. Jesus' death and resurrection (providing an option for us to return to God) further indicate how precious the freedom to choose is. Clearly, an authentic, non-coercive relationship between God and people is something to be treasured above anything else.

Question 7: **How would you explain the correlation between separation from God and the entrance of evil and suffering into the world?** Humankind sinned, which produced an immediate separation from God. Evil and suffering were a direct result. After our rebellion "all hell broke loose"—literally. The evil around us is both the consequence of our rebellion and a taste of what is to come for those who want a world in which God is entirely absent. (The Bible calls that world hell.)

Question 8: **Share your opinion of the following statement: "God cannot both create human beings with a total ability to freely make meaningful choices and at the same time control them so they always choose good."** Some people in your group may agree with this statement because exercising free will means by definition that people are not programmed to always choose good. Others in your group may disagree, saying that God could and should have given us free will and at the same time put in us a compelling desire to want only what is right and good.

Question 9: **Do you consider your freedom of choice to be a gift from God? Why or why not? What would human relationships be like without free will?** This question is asking if the freedom to choose is something your group members value, or if they would prefer a robotlike existence. We think most people will see the value in being human and free rather than mere automatons. Since that is how an all-wise God created us, it seems consistent with his view and the better of the two options.

Question 10: If you could eliminate all evil, suffering, and sin (wrongdoing) in your life by giving up your free will, would you do it? Explain.

Question 11: Do you ever become angry at God for the things that go wrong in your life? Why or why not? It is perfectly natural to feel anger toward God when we don't understand life. The Bible is full of examples of people openly and honestly bringing out their confusion and venting at God. The Psalms, inspired by the Holy Spirit, are full of such lament. This question can give you the opportunity to help your group members see that it is appropriate to bring their problems and feelings right out in the open before God. He is willing and able to handle their concerns, even when they are presented "imperfectly."

Question 12: Check the statement(s) below [see guide] that best describes your position at this point. Share your selection with the rest of the group and give reasons for your response.

DISCUSSION TWO

Why Do Innocent People Suffer?

Short Answer: People suffer because we live in a sin-stained world. However, in one sense there are no truly innocent people, so no truly innocent people suffer. Yet it is the very nature of evil to not discriminate among its victims, which is why evil is so volatile and dangerous.

Question 1: Share a personal example of a time when you or someone close to you experienced suffering for no just reason.

Question 2: Do you agree with the following Bible passage [see guide], which teaches that evil people flourish and the innocent suffer? Give examples to support your answer.

Question 3: Which source(s) produced the suffering you described in question 1? Based on these categories [see guide], where do your feelings of blame or anger get directed? Explain.

Question 4: When tornadoes, earthquakes, floods, disease, and other acts of nature cause tremendous suffering in the lives of people, which of the explanations listed below [see guide] seem reasonable to you? Why?

Question 5: If God isn't directly controlling everything that happens, what's a reasonable explanation for natural disasters? God set natural laws in place and doesn't normally interfere as they take their course. When sin entered the picture, those natural laws continued to operate but with some distortion. Disasters are not caused by some sort of meddling by God; rather disasters are due to this mutilation of nature.

Question 6: Describe a time when you in some way caused or deserved the suffering you were experiencing. Did you still tend to want to blame someone or something other than yourself? Why? We often react to pain with the knee-jerk reaction of blame, even if we ourselves are the ones responsible. Often God is the one we get mad at, despite the reality that he may have had nothing at all to do with the hardship.

Question 7: Considering the pain we bring upon ourselves, why do you think God admonishes us in the Bible to "hate what is evil; cling to what is good" (Romans 12:9)? God's guidelines given to us in the Bible are designed to keep us from hurting God, others, or ourselves. His blueprint for living is not a way to keep us from enjoying life but instead leads to life without regret or unneeded pain.

Question 8: In light of humankind's rejection of God and his ways, what point do you think C. S. Lewis is trying to get across when he states, "The question is not 'Why do the innocent suffer?' but rather 'Why don't we all suffer more?'" Do you agree with him? Why or why not? The point C. S. Lewis is making is that based on the choices we have made to reject God, it seems consistent that we ought to be experiencing more suffering and evil than we do. It is only by God's goodness and grace that we have not already received what is justly due for the sins we've committed.

Question 9: Can you think of any positive things that come out of our suffering? Share a personal example if you have

one. In case some members of your group have difficulty identifying positive results of suffering, be prepared to give an example from your own life.

Question 10: How do you suppose it's possible to love someone yet deny them something they really want (and you have the ability to provide)? Give examples.

Question 11: Has God ever used pain and suffering in your life to get your attention? What was he attempting to get across to you?

Question 12: What possible alternatives to pain and suffering could God have used to capture your attention? Would they have been as effective? You may want to point out that the alternatives suggested by the members of your group might not capture our attention in quite the same way that pain and suffering would. For example, clearly spelled-out warnings in the Bible seem to easily go unheeded. And if the pain is not strong enough, we will most likely ignore it. Without the sensation of pain, a child might be tempted to touch the flames of a fire and not reflexively pull away—resulting in irreparable destruction of tissue. In that sense, pain is a gift to keep us from actions that destroy the body. Likewise, guilt can also be a gift that urges us to stop other destructive behaviors.

Question 13: In what ways can the truth of these verses [see guide] bring comfort in the suffering you endure?

Question 14: Check the statement(s) below [see guide] that best describes your position at this point. Share your selection with the rest of the group and give reasons for your response.

DISCUSSION THREE

Why Doesn't God Do Something?

Short Answer: He has done something through Jesus Christ; this act must hold us over until, at the end of time, he rights every wrong.

Question 1: Have you ever wished that God would step in and rewrite the ending to a story in your life or the life of someone close to you? Share an example. Use this question to allow group members to open up to each other about their lives. Doing so will build bridges of trust and support for one another. Be sure to encourage the personal side of the group experience. A small group is not just a class but rather an opportunity for authentic openness and real life-change to occur.

Question 2: How do you think God would answer Habakkuk's accusations?

Question 3: What does Habakkuk's ability to raise these issues with God (and their inclusion in the Bible) tell you about God's openness to tough questions directed at him? Here you may want to point out that the Bible itself doesn't ignore these kinds of tough questions. Habakkuk wondered about the same perplexing issues we face today.

Question 4: Listed below is a set of scenarios [see guide] describing how God could respond to the problem of suffering and evil. Select the one you like best and give some reasons for your selection. Which ones do you think are *not* good options?

Question 5: Suppose God did step in and wipe out every trace of evil. In light of Romans 3:23 ("All have sinned and fall short of the glory of God"), what would that do to the human population? Where would that leave you? The implication is that all of us would be wiped out in such a sweeping removal of evil.

Question 6: If there were no sin (wrongdoing) in the world, do you think there would be any suffering and evil? Why or why not?

Question 7: Given the above quote [see guide], why wouldn't it have been better if God had created us without an ability to choose evil in the first place? Group members may suggest that one possible option would be for God to give us the freedom to choose, but limit our choices to only good ones. That, however, is an impossibility because it produces a contradiction in terms—there is no real choice if there is no possibility for more than one option.

Question 8: **What insight does this verse [see guide] give concerning one reason why God currently tolerates evil?** God seems to be patiently waiting for all of us to take advantage of the opportunity to choose him. He tolerates evil for the sake of those who've not yet come to him, which means his patience with evil is not some sort of weakness or indecision but rather a gracious act of compassion toward those who've not yet repented.

Question 9: **What advantages are there in allowing people to see evil firsthand and then inviting them to reject it in favor of living under God's leadership? Do you believe this is the best way to deal with evil? Why or why not?** Because God allows people to experience evil firsthand, we are exposed a little to what life is like without God. Once we've seen this, we can make a more educated choice about whether we want to be separated from his goodness for eternity. Although this is a conjecture, perhaps through humanity's failure the whole universe is learning a lesson that could serve worlds and beings yet to be created!

Question 10: **If you knew for sure that God would rid the world of evil somehow, in his own time, and bring about absolute justice, how would you feel about having to tolerate evil and suffering now?** Even knowing that evil may someday be wiped out doesn't necessarily reduce the pain and suffering being experienced now. Here's a good time to express sincere concern for the hardships any group members are currently facing.

Question 11: **What is your reaction to the claim that Jesus Christ, out of his great love for you, died on your behalf to pay the penalty for the evil in your life?** Give your group members the freedom to express their doubts about whether they believe this claim. In any case, try to encourage them to answer the question hypothetically, assuming for the sake of discussion that the claim is true.

Question 12: If Jesus Christ and his death for you were all God gave you to help you cope with evil in your life, would that be enough? What else would you need? Here's an opportunity to point out that God gives believers the Holy Spirit (John 16:5–15) who, among other things, provides comfort, strength, and encouragement during difficult times (John 14:25–27).

Question 13: Check the statement(s) below [see guide] that best describes your position at this point. Share your selection with the rest of the group and give reasons for your response.

DISCUSSION FOUR

Is the Devil for Real?

Short Answer: Yes, he is a fallen angel in rebellion against God and seeks to gather other people into his web of defiance.

Question 1: Growing up, what did you believe about the devil? What most influenced your thinking?

Question 2: Do you currently believe that an evil spiritual being exists? Why or why not? What is the value of trying to find out if such a being exists? Hopefully, group members will see the relevancy of this topic. Determining the reality of an evil spiritual being raises the awareness level needed to take the devil seriously, which in turn enables effective use of countermeasures.

Question 3: What difference does it make to you that Jesus believed in the devil? What other evidence for the devil's existence could be put forward? Because of the credibility of Jesus (argued in another guide), his statements about the devil should be taken seriously. In some ways, knowing that Jesus believed in the devil ends the discussion, because if Jesus is the trustworthy Son of God, would *you* want to accuse him of error?

Question 4: What did the devil seem to want from Jesus [in Matthew 4:1–11], and what tactics did he employ? How

did Jesus get the devil to leave him alone? The devil wanted Jesus to listen to him and obey him. The devil used Scripture to tempt Jesus to submit to his challenges, but Jesus resisted him by quoting God's Word back to him.

Question 5: **The devil first shows up in the Bible in the Garden of Eden. As described in the following passage from Genesis [3:1–5], how does the devil try to get Eve to accept a distorted picture of God? Do you think Satan uses these same tactics today?** The devil took the words of God and twisted and distorted them in an attempt to confuse and deceive Eve. God hadn't said they couldn't eat from *any* tree; rather he said there was *one* tree to avoid and the rest were allowed. Satan greatly exaggerated the command to make God's request seem unreasonable. He also called God a liar and painted a picture of a stingy, overbearing God. Satan's temptation was not ultimately about the fruit; it was about getting Eve to accept a distorted picture of God. That was Satan's ultimate aim and it remains his goal to this day. R. C. Sproul says, "Satan is described as an accuser, a liar, and a tempter. We see him lying, distorting the truth, we see him involved in temptation, and we see him accusing the saints."

Question 6: **If the devil is an intelligent but rebellious angel, what do you think his motives are in trying to trip up people and gain additional "God rejecters" among humans?** Misery loves company! The devil's very rejection of God means he would enjoy seeing others share in that rejection. (He is happy to allow this rejection of God to masquerade as neutrality toward God. Jesus warned, "He who is not with me is against me, and he who does not gather with me scatters" [Matthew 12:30]).

Question 7: **What role might Satan play in the evil and suffering experienced in our world today?** For reasons not totally clear, God has allowed Satan a certain amount of freedom to cause trouble here on earth. Some of the evil and suffering we experience is a direct result of Satan's attacks on us.

Question 8: According to the verses below [see guide], what is the extent of the devil's power? What do you think about the fairness of this situation? Even though God has allowed the devil to exercise power on this earth, God has limited that power and remains in ultimate control.

Question 9: Why do you suppose God doesn't just eliminate Satan now? The Bible does not give a clear answer to this question. It seems that God is waiting to bring judgment to Satan and the world at a later time. Possibly God is giving each of us more time to gain a better understanding of who we are choosing to side with (Satan) if we continue to reject our Creator and God. Also see question 8 of discussion three in this guide for additional insights.

Question 10: What is your emotional response to the possibility of the devil's existence? What would help you determine, one way or the other, what the truth is concerning the devil?

Question 11: Put into your own words the meaning behind what the Bible recommends in the following passages [see guide] as defense against the devil.

Question 12: Check the statement(s) below [see guide] that best describes your position at this point. Share your selection with the rest of the group and give reasons for your response.

DISCUSSION FIVE

How Could a Loving God Send People to Hell?

Short Answer: He doesn't; people send themselves to hell by ignoring the one willing to receive and forgive. A loving God is doing everything he can to get people to stop their stubborn resistance.

Question 1: What is your position concerning the concept of hell? Choose from the statements below [see guide] and give an explanation for your choice(s).

Question 2: On what basis have you come to your conclusions about hell? Which of the sources listed below [see guide] strongly influence the position you take?

Question 3: How dependable are your sources of authority for your understanding about the idea of a hell? Use a scale from one to ten to indicate your response (one being a weak level of reliability and ten being a very strong level of reliability).

Question 4: On what basis do the people listed above [see guide] believe or not believe that an actual place called hell exists? How does the reliability of their sources compare with the reliability of yours? People who examine the sources of their beliefs about hell may discover they have inadequate reasons for their views. This discovery may spur them on to getting a better foundation for what they believe about such an important topic—especially in light of the subject's eternal ramifications!

Question 5: Based on the verses listed above [see guide], what are some of the reasons the Bible gives for why people end up in hell? Ultimately, the reason people wind up in hell is not because God sent them there but because people prefer hell to submission to God. Hell is the ultimate separation from God. It is the eternal destiny that logically follows a lifetime of choosing to omit God from one's life. Jesus wept over Jerusalem, wanting—longing—to gather the inhabitants to himself, but like so many others throughout time, *they were unwilling.* As you participate in the group discussion, be sure to bring these points out if those in your group do not.

Question 6: Based on the verses listed above [see guide], what observations can you make about what hell is really like? The Bible seems to be teaching that hell is a literal and actual place. The torments are emotional (regret), spiritual (separation from God), and probably even physical (burning). Whatever the specifics, hell is an utterly horrible place described in the Bible with a variety of dreadfully negative analogies.

Question 7: What do you think of the following objections to the idea of hell [see guide]? Can you come up with some of your own?

Question 8: What is your reaction to the assertions listed above [see guide]? Which ideas do you agree with and which do you disagree with? What conclusions can be drawn about God's desire concerning everyone's eternal destiny?

Question 9: How do you feel about the hope that evil will not last forever? The existence of hell can be a kind of good news, especially to those who have suffered at the hands of others. It's the place where God tells the victim, "I will confine your enemy here so he can't hurt you anymore"; where he tells all those who've suffered under oppression, "Those who didn't treat you as human won't be allowed to continue in their wicked ways anymore." Finally all moral pollution is contained so no one has to suffer the consequences of those who refuse to give up their evil ways.

Question 10: Do you think that when people avoid or reject God and his involvement in their lives, they realize they are actually choosing hell? On a more personal level, have *you* resisted God at times in your life? Explain. People do not usually realize that resisting God is actually distancing themselves from him, which is a foretaste of the ultimate separation from God found in hell. We trivialize our resistance to God, thinking that we have a better way (which is usually why we resist God). The reality is that God's ways are always best, even though in the short run we don't always see why.

Question 11: Can hell, God's justice, and God's love all be real and true at the same time? Explain. Hell is God's way of preserving human dignity. He recognizes and honors the right of people to choose, including the right to reject a relationship with him. His justice is shown not in overlooking sin but in enforcing its consequences and honoring people's choices. His love is shown in sending his Son as payment for sin, providing an opportunity for humankind to come back to God. Also, because of his great love for us, God has clearly warned about the destination awaiting those who continue to live distanced from him.

Question 12: Check the statement(s) below [see guide] that best describes your position at this point. Share your selection with the rest of the group and give reasons for your response.

DISCUSSION SIX

Is There Really a Heaven?

Short Answer: Yes, and we have the awesome privilege of enjoying its beauty and splendor if we choose to let Jesus Christ forgive our sins so we can have a right relationship with God and go there.

Question 1: Do you believe there is some kind of life after death? What reasons do you have for your answer?

Question 2: Which of the following options [see guide] do you believe happens after death? What influenced your thinking?

Question 3: Which of the concerns or questions listed below [see guide] have you had as you've thought about heaven?

Question 4: What do the phrases "many rooms" and "prepare a place" convey to you about the personal touches and loving concern Jesus says await you in heaven? How might this teaching address fears about heaven being boring? Jesus' words about heaven assure us of at least two things: First, it must exist if an authority of the stature of Jesus says so. Second, if he is preparing a place for us, it must be a wonderful and personal place, because someone of Jesus' power and love is behind its creation (for at least two thousand years now!) and adaptation for us.

Question 5: If we have to be good to enter heaven, how good do we have to be? Can anyone know for sure if he or she has been good enough? The point of this question is to expose people's ideas of what it takes to enter heaven. The standard that God has set for people to enter heaven is perfection. That standard is too high for anyone to measure up (Romans 3:23), which means no one can enter heaven based on good deeds alone (Titus 3:5). Unless you have a perfect record, forgiveness is required to get into heaven (Romans 6:23).

Question 6: **According to your understanding of the Bible, on what basis do sinful people gain entrance into heaven? Do you believe people can be confident that they're going to heaven? Why or why not?** People gain entrance into heaven because of the payment Jesus made when he died for our sins. When people place their faith and trust in what Christ has done in paying that penalty, they can be absolutely confident that they are restored into a relationship with God and will enter heaven in the hereafter.

Question 7: **How confident are you that you will spend eternity in heaven? What is the basis for your level of confidence?** This question provides a great opportunity for you to discover where the members of your group are spiritually. Use it as a chance to help people see their need to accept Jesus Christ into their lives. For those who have received salvation but are doubting, remind them that if they have trusted Christ, their entering heaven is now a matter of Christ's trustworthiness; it's not based on anything else they can do (or fail to do). They can have confidence in their destination, based on the promises of God (1 John 5:11–13; Romans 5:8).

Question 8: **What difference does it make to have assurance now about where you'll spend eternity?**

Question 9: **Although God doesn't promise you freedom from pain in this life, is it enough that he offers to be with you now and care for you forever in a place totally void of evil and suffering, called heaven? Why or why not?**

Question 10: **At this point in your spiritual journey, how important is the concept of heaven to you?** Although time spent thinking about heaven has been criticized as diverting one's attention from critical matters at hand on earth, confidence in someday going to heaven can lead to a peace and calmness that brings great comfort now. Knowing your future is settled can help you to live with greater freedom, and knowing there's a better day ahead can keep you going when the going gets tough.

Question 11: Check the statement(s) below [see guide] that best describes your position at this point. Share your selection with the rest of the group and give reasons for your response.

CHAPTER FIVE

Don't All Religions Lead to God?

DISCUSSION ONE

Don't All Religions Teach Basically the Same Thing?

Short Answer: No. After careful examination, major differences of doctrine and practice exist, especially as compared with Christianity.

Question 1: Why do you think there are so many religions in the world?

Question 2: Do you think all major religions are **fundamentally the same or fundamentally different? If you can, give reasons to back up your answer.** Many of your group members will probably comment that the major religions are basically the same. Their reasons might include things like: all religions promote goodwill toward others and God. At this point accept everybody's comments; don't be tempted to argue against this way of thinking.

Question 3: **True or false: If a religion inspires people to live better lives, we shouldn't question it. Explain your reasoning.** The purpose of this question is to raise the issue that even though a religion might inspire people to live their lives well—which is a good thing—it might not contain the truth about how to find a relationship with God. The religion may very well only improve some aspect of life now, without providing for eternity—which would be a terrible tragedy. As Greg Koukl concludes, "If issues of religion have eternal consequences, then errors in thinking are infinitely tragic.

To rephrase Karl Marx, false religion is the opiate of the people. It soothes, but does not cure" *(Clear Thinking)*.

Question 4: **What difference, if any, would it make if the source of an idea or concept of great value to you was false?**

Question 5: **True or false: People who claim to have the only truth about religion are arrogant, and such conceited attitudes are the cause of great strife and conflict in the world. Give an explanation for your answer.** There are times when people do claim, in an arrogant and conceited way, to have the only truth about religion. This attitude probably exists with some members of all religions, but it wouldn't be reason enough necessarily to discredit any one religion. A person's arrogance can, however, cause others to be less open to his or her particular religion.

Question 6: **How does the above legend [see guide] apply to the issue of searching for and finding the truth about God and religion? Do you agree with its conclusion? Why or why not?** It may seem fitting—and even logical—that each of us in the world has a small piece of the total truth, and that is what explains all the different religions in the world. That analogy breaks down, however, when you consider the poem regarding the blind men and the elephant. In it the men are all groping for the truth yet finding only pieces of it. But if the elephant could talk and reveal what he was like to the blind men, they would have more of the total picture. Christianity is not blind men reaching for God (as is the case with man-made religions); it is God coming to blind men to clearly explain himself in Christ. In Christianity the "elephant" tells us who he is and what he's like.

Question 7: **How likely does it seem to you that any one religion would have the final say on what is true or not? Explain.**

Question 8: **Does it seem reasonable to expect all religions to be true in their own way, in spite of significant differences? Why or why not?** The idea that one should accept all religions in spite of differences is a very popular view called pluralism. The problem with this way of thinking is that it defies logic and reasoning. Two things that contradict each other cannot both be true at the same time. Tolerance, which says we should accept people even if we reject their ideas, is commendable; but pluralism, which says everyone is right, is impossible and dishonest. Grantley Morris adds, "To overlook obvious differences between religions might seem broad-minded. In reality it is about as proud and narrow as a person could get. To say all religions are basically the same is to claim to be smarter than each of the billions of people who believe the unique aspects of their religion are of supreme importance to God. It is to claim that even though you are not an expert in their religion, you know they are wrong—you know their religion is really no different."

Question 9: **Explain the significant differences behind the following two motivations for belief [see guide].** The significant difference between these two statements is the credibility of the one promoting the belief. In the first statement, personal opinion is the proof; in the second, the authority is Jesus Christ himself, not the one who holds the belief. (Note: The credibility of Jesus is addressed in another guide in this series, *What Difference Does Jesus Make?*)

Question 10: **What is the difference between *toleration* of all religions and *validation* of all religions?** Tolerance promotes the freedom to believe whatever a person wants to believe. Validation promotes the acceptance of a religion as true, or valid.

Question 11: **Do you think that for one religion to be true, all other religions must be *completely* false? (Do you think the six men in the Indian legend were each *completely* wrong?) Explain.** Christianity doesn't teach that every religion has *only* falsehood; rather it claims that although some truth may be found there, no other religion began with God's initiative and provides the true way to rescue people from the plight sin brings.

Question 12: Do Christianity's exclusive claims worry, bother, or embarrass you? How has your reaction changed over time? Explain.

Question 13: Is it confusing or frustrating to you that there are so many different religions from which to choose? Why or why not? It may be frustrating to some members of your group that God would allow so many different religions. Give them the freedom to express these feelings.

Question 14: If religions are all different, why do you think God allows so many of them to exist? Why doesn't he just narrow down the choices so it's easier to find him? To do that, God would have to step in and take away our freedom of choice, which the Bible tells us he is not about to do. So he allows false religion, even as he allows people to make other poor choices. In the midst of the confusion stands the teaching and work of Jesus, a shining light in the darkness. His lighthouse is pointing the way, even though many ignore it.

Question 15: On a scale from one to ten, place an *X* near the spot and phrase [see guide] that best describes your position at this point. Share your selection with the rest of the group and give reasons for placing your *X* where you did.

DISCUSSION TWO

Isn't It Enough to Be Sincere?

Short Answer: No. It is possible to be sincerely wrong; therefore it is important to be both sincere and right.

Question 1: Think of a conversation in which someone was insincere with you. How did you feel about that interaction? Why is sincerity in relationships so important? This question is designed to expose the frustration most people have about insincerity, especially insincerity within religion. While insincerity is not a good thing, neither is sincerity within falsehood. The goal is to help people see the need to be sincere and correct.

Question 2: Do you think that ultimately, no matter what we believe about God, we will all end up at the same place as long as we are sincere in what we believe? What is the basis for your answer? This question hits at the popular view that no matter what people believe, it is okay as long as they are sincere. By the end of this session, group members should get the idea that this way of thinking cannot logically be correct.

Question 3: Have you experienced a situation in which someone you know was sincere but sincerely wrong? Briefly tell about it. What makes that experience so tragic?

Question 4: Suppose that in the realm of religion, the only thing that mattered was sincerity. What would be the benefits of such a system? What might be some disadvantages? One advantage might be the relative simplicity of the system. But it would lead to great harm in almost every area of life, because truth—reality—would no longer matter. The world would become a nightmare, with every action justified by sincerity. In addition, how does one measure sincerity and how much sincerity is necessary? Is anyone totally sincere? Aren't we all a mixed bag in this regard? Also, a God of justice would be a joke; there would be no justice, only sincerity.

Question 5: Consider the following statement: "One who does a good deed with an evil motive is an evil person, and one who does an evil deed by accident with a good motive is not an evil person." Do you agree? Why or why not? Both sincerity and good actions matter. One without the other leads to problems.

Question 6: Do you agree or disagree with the archbishop's response [see guide]? What role does sincerity play in determining the truth behind these statements? A person's sincere belief, one way or the other, does not affect the essence of the truth. An apple is a fruit. One person may eat it and like it, and another person may not. But the apple does not stop being a fruit just because someone doesn't like it. Abraham Lincoln once quipped, "Suppose you call a tail a leg.

How many legs does a dog have? The answer is four; calling a tail a leg doesn't make it one." (Interesting note: It has been reported that Jane Fonda has since accepted Christ as her personal savior.)

Question 7: Anatole France once said, "If 50 million people believe a foolish thing, it is still a foolish thing." Would it make any difference if the 50 million people had sincere intentions? Explain. Sincerity makes error into a tragedy, not a truth.

Question 8: Based on the above illustration [see guide], someone can be sincerely wrong. Do you believe that this conclusion also applies to one's religion and relationship with God? What exceptions or comparisons can you identify? Explain. Cliffe Knechtle states, "Truth matters when you go take a test. The Day of Judgment will be the final exam when you and I will stand before God and have to give an account for all of our actions, all of our words, all of our thoughts. And the question is, are you ready for that final exam?" *(Give Me an Answer).*

Question 9: Do you find that some people in your world (neighborhood, business, family, etc.) often have an insincere streak but don't always see it in themselves? Explain.

Question 10: What about you? Is it important for you to be sincere in all your dealings? What tempts you to *not* be sincere?

Question 11: Do you have any fears about being sincerely wrong about your spiritual beliefs? Explain.

Question 12: To what degree are you interested in sincerely basing your beliefs on the truth? How difficult is that for you to do? Explain.

Question 13: Check the statement(s) below [see guide] that best describes your position at this point. Share your selection with the rest of the group and give reasons for your response.

Question 14: On a scale from one to ten, place an X near the spot and phrase [see guide] that best describes your position at this point. Share your selection with the rest of the group and give reasons for placing your X where you did.

DISCUSSION THREE

What's So Different About Christianity?

Short Answer: Christianity is the only religion that teaches that salvation is a gift from God offered through Jesus Christ, not something a person can earn by following a set of religious guidelines.

Question 1: Do you know anyone who is a faithful follower of any of the major world religions other than Christianity (Buddhism, Hinduism, Islam, or Judaism)? What characterizes someone who practices that particular religion?

Question 2: Give a one- or two-sentence summary of what you know about one of the following major world religions: Hinduism, Buddhism, Islam, or Judaism.

Question 3: To what extent do (and should) the scripture of a religion and the credibility of its founder influence your willingness to accept its teachings? What other factors attract you to—or repel you from—a religion? It would seem that the credibility of both the scripture and the founder should matter a great deal. It is interesting that many followers of religions do not make this a priority for validating what they devote themselves to. Often, more superficial factors such as social convention, benefits derived from membership, subjective experiences and feelings from participating in the group, and current leadership (a charismatic person in charge of the local assembly) are more convincing.

Question 4: Describe some differences you notice in the basic beliefs and teachings among the above five religions [see guide]. (Include any other differences you know of that are not on the chart.) How significant do these differences seem to you?

Question 5: **Do you think it is possible that all five of these religions are teaching truth? Why or why not? How do these religions address meaning-of-life issues (life's problems and life's answers)?** Each of the five major world religions may have some truth to them, but when they are promoting teachings that logically contradict each other, they cannot all be representing the truth. They describe radically different Gods (or no God at all), radically different ways to connect with God (or find ultimate meaning), and radically different lifestyles that reflect God's character.

Question 6: **What do you observe as a common link among all four of these religions [see guide], especially concerning how a person obtains salvation?** All four of these religions teach that salvation is obtained through a process of performing certain duties. In all these belief systems salvation is earned, not a free gift.

Question 7: **To what extent could a person be confident that he or she has measured up to the required standards of any of these four religions [see guide]? Explain.** There is always an element of ambiguity with such systems: "Have I done enough?" "Was my wrong too wrong?" You never know where you stand. This uncertainty usually leaves people frustrated and fearful.

Question 8: **How do the other world religions contrast or compare with the above outline of salvation from the teachings of Christianity [see guide]?** The thing that sets Christianity apart from all other religions is that Christianity clearly states that we all have a sin problem which is only completely resolved through Jesus Christ's offer of forgiveness and reconciliation. This provision of salvation is a gift, not something that can be earned. C. S. Lewis points out that Christianity's founder, Jesus Christ, is the only religious leader who made claims to deity:

> There is no half-way house, and there is no parallel in other religions. If you had gone to Buddha and asked, "Are you the son of Bramah?" he would have said, "You

are still in a veil of illusion." If you had gone to Socrates and asked, "Are you Zeus?" he would have laughed at you. If you had gone to Mohammed and asked, "Are you Allah?" He would first have rent his clothes and then cut your head off. If you asked Confucius, "Are you heaven?" I think he probably would have replied: "Remarks which are not in accordance with nature are in bad taste." The idea of a great moral teacher saying what Christ said is out of the question. In my opinion, the only person who can say that sort of thing is either God or a complete lunatic suffering from that form of delusion which undermines the whole mind of man.

—*God in the Dock*

Question 9: **Are you aware of any evidence that shows that reincarnation (the transmigration of souls into new forms after death, based on karma) occurs? Do you think Hinduism or Buddhism would make sense if reincarnation was *not* true? Why or why not?** It is amazing to think that people would believe in reincarnation when there is no evidence for it. Even if you put forward supposed past-life regressions and memories of those lives, reincarnation teaches that we come back as animals and inanimate objects—where's the evidence for that? Much is at stake here because without reincarnation, Buddhism and Hinduism cannot stand.

Question 10: **Which of the five major religions summarized in this lesson make sense to you? Which makes the most sense? The least?**

Question 11: **How do you feel about the fact that people believe so differently—and strongly—when it comes to religion? What reasons can you give for these differences?** Many people feel that their religion is not necessarily something they choose for themselves but something determined by the culture in which they are raised. While that may be true experientially, it is not a good way to proceed with such an important decision. People may become entrenched in their belief systems because change is uncomfortable. It's a frightening thing to face one's errors—who enjoys admitting they've been wrong?—yet we all need to know and understand *why* we believe whatever we believe. God holds us accountable for the light (or knowledge) we've been given and what we've done with it.

Question 12: On what will you base your decision as to which religion, if any, is right for you?

Question 13: On a scale from one to ten, place an *X* near the spot and phrase [see guide] that best describes you. Share your selection with the rest of the group and give reasons for placing your *X* where you did.

DISCUSSION FOUR

Aren't Mormons and Jehovah's Witnesses Christians, Too?

Short Answer: No. Despite some similarities, the teachings of both Mormons and Jehovah's Witnesses are not consistent with historical, biblical Christianity on major points of belief and practice.

Question 1: What's your reaction to people who proselytize (try to convert others to their religion)?

Question 2: How would you describe people you know who were raised in (or converted to) the Mormon or Jehovah's Witnesses religions? It's important to humanize members of these faiths. They are people just like you and me who've gotten caught in a theological system of half-truths and error.

Question 3: What do you think Mormons and Jehovah's Witnesses have in common with other Christian believers? What have you discovered to be distinguishing beliefs and/or practices of Mormons and Jehovah's Witnesses? This question will help you, as the leader, to know how familiar your group members are with these groups. In *So What's the Difference?* Fritz Ridenour has the following to say about the Jehovah's Witnesses: "Jehovah's Witnesses are a challenge to Christians for several reasons: (1) Most of their growth has taken place just recently; (2) they will probably continue growing because they preach their message to a world on the brink of nuclear war; (3) their teachings are flatly opposed to the gospel; (4) they are flatly opposed to the Christian church, which they say is of the devil; (5) they deny the deity of Jesus Christ, the person and work of the Holy Spirit and many other vital doctrines; and (6) they claim that their teachings are the only real truth about the Bible." And Walter Martin, in *Kingdom of the Cults,* states about the Mormons, "One can search the corridors of pagan mythology and never equal the complex structure which the Mormons have erected and masked under the terminology and misnomer of orthodox Christianity."

Question 4: **How would you define a cult? Do you think the Mormons or the Jehovah's Witnesses fall into your definition of a cult? Why or why not?**

Question 5: **Do you agree or disagree with these diagnostic questions to identify a cult [see guide]? Explain.** When you discuss the first criteria of a cult, its distortion of Christ, this would include denial of the doctrine of the Trinity, denial of his bodily resurrection, and erroneous views about his second coming. Errors about Christ are the most serious because he is the key to our salvation and understanding of God (John 8:24).

Question 6: **Review the information in the above two Straight Talks about the Mormons and the Jehovah's Witnesses [see guide]. What makes their teachings and doctrines very different from the Bible's teachings?** The main differences are in who Christ is and what saves us. Note: Some of the members of your group may feel intimidated if they don't know enough about the Bible to make knowledgeable statements. Assure those who are struggling that at this point in their spiritual journey, it's okay to learn about this topic one step at a time—everybody has to start somewhere!

Question 7: What facts most intrigue you about the above two religions [see guide]? What is appealing—or unappealing—to you about Mormonism and Jehovah's Witnesses?

Question 8: In your opinion, are the differences between the Mormon and the Jehovah's Witnesses religions and Christianity significant enough for these two religions to warrant the label "cult"? Why or why not? If what is meant by "cult" is a group whose members live radical, out-of-the-mainstream lifestyles, these groups don't fit that definition—their members are found throughout our society. But if by "cult" one means a group which teaches that it exclusively embodies Christianity, yet deviates in significant ways from biblical Christian teaching, then both the Mormons and the Jehovah's Witnesses would fall into that category.

Question 9: What, in your view, explains how a group can misstate biblical truths and teach such different doctrines yet produce people who in most respects seem "Christian" in their behavior? Because the Bible is a major source (among others) of the teachings of both the Mormons and the Jehovah's Witnesses, similarities of moral practice exist. Besides, nowhere in the Bible does it state that only followers of the true faith have external goodness. Lots of people live exemplary lives—even atheists. What's missing from anyone outside the sphere of Christ is forgiveness of sin.

Question 10: What "fruit" besides living a good life could Jesus have been referring to when he distinguished between true and false teachers (or prophets) by saying, "By their fruit you will recognize them" (Matthew 7:15–23)? Jesus was also referring to the effects of their doctrinal teachings. A false prophet could gather followers and turn them into nice people who defer to the cult leader for truth instead of to Christ and the Bible. These followers usually have a false assurance of salvation because they are not being led into a true relationship with God through Jesus Christ. Consider having your group read Matthew 7:15–23 together.

Question 11: How does it make you feel when you hear Christians say that the Mormons and the Jehovah's Witnesses are cults or sects? Is this spiritual bigotry? Explain your answer. To label a religion as a cult or sect is not spiritual bigotry if the designation is made after careful examination of the teachings of that religion. Bigotry assumes you're saying something unfair about someone's character. Labeling a group a spiritual counterfeit says nothing about the moral qualities of the people in that group; it speaks only about the group's teachings.

Question 12: How do you explain why the Mormons and the Jehovah's Witnesses are growing in such large numbers? If a group is not in harmony with the Bible's teachings, why do you think God would let it have increasing influence?

Question 13: If sincere members of groups like these can be mistaken in their fundamental beliefs, what assurance do you have that you are correct about *your* beliefs? Can anyone really know for sure that he or she is right? Explain your answer.

Question 14: On a scale from one to ten, place an X near the spot and phrase [see guide] that best describes you. Share your selection with the rest of the group and give reasons for placing your X where you did.

DISCUSSION FIVE

Is Jesus Really the Only Way to God?

Short Answer: Yes. Jesus Christ claimed to be the *only* one who, through his death and resurrection, is able to forgive sinners and bring people into a relationship with God.

Question 1: What is your immediate reaction to the claim that Jesus Christ is the only way to God? How do you suppose most people react to this claim?

Question 2: What are some objections that come to mind concerning the claim that Jesus is the only way? Describe a path of salvation that is *not* exclusive and that would make more sense to those troubled by the "one way" proposal. There are a number of reasons why people cannot accept that Jesus Christ is the only way to God. Perhaps the strongest argument is that there are too many people who do not believe in Jesus Christ who would therefore be excluded from God. The exclusivity of Christianity troubles many people because it seems unfair to deny those who believe differently access to God and his blessings.

Question 3: Do you think the Bible specifically teaches that Jesus is the only way to God? Why? Cite a couple examples to support your answer, if possible.

Question 4: Select *one* of the Bible passages from the list below [see guide] and put it into your own words.

Question 5: Based on the above list of Scripture passages [see guide], explain your reaction to the following statement: "Christianity does not claim that Jesus is the only way to God." Some people assume that only Christians—not Christ and not the Bible—claim that Jesus is the only way to God. This question is designed to expose this misunderstanding by looking at the Scriptures, which clearly teach that Jesus and the Bible make that astonishing claim.

Question 6: Assuming Christianity does indeed assert that Jesus is the only way, what reasons might people give for viewing this claim as false?

Question 7: Each of the above objections [see guide] is based on unspoken assumptions about how one determines what is true. Match each objection listed above with its corresponding assumption listed below [see guide]. Explain your answer. Here are the corresponding assumptions matched to each objection listed in the Straight Talk "Three Common Objections": (1) popular opinion defines truth; (2) intensity of belief ensures truth; and (3) anything intolerant negates truth.

Question 8: Do you think the above assumptions [see guide] are still true in light of the contradicting observations? How does your answer apply to similar truths in the spiritual realm? The illustrations given in the Straight Talk "Three Assumptions Examined" clearly show that the cultural assumptions about truth are not correct. There is no good reason to accept these erroneous assumptions in the spiritual realm either.

Question 9: **If Jesus was not who he claimed to be (the only way to God), which of the other alternatives listed above [see guide] seems most reasonable to you? Why?** Because Jesus specifically claimed that he was the only way to God, the only logical conclusion is that Jesus was either a liar, a lunatic, a made-up legend, or the truth. If he is not the truth, the only possibilities are the remaining three (*Beyond Blind Faith*, Paul E. Little).

Question 10: **How does concluding that there is more than one way to God make a mockery out of Christ's death?** If there is more than one way to God, Christ's death was not really necessary. In a sense he died in vain, because there were other ways to God all along. But the Bible claims just the opposite, that Jesus died and rose again because it was the only hope of the world. Sin must be dealt with, and Christ is the way God has bridged the "sin gap."

Question 11: **If Jesus Christ really is the only way to God, what impact would wholeheartedly believing this have on our lives and relationships?** Use this question to help your group members come to grips with their own relationship with God, and with talking to others about knowing him. Members of your group may want to take the step of asking Christ into their lives at this point in the series. Others may begin to take seriously their need to figure out how to creatively share the Christian message with friends and family.

Question 12: **On a scale from one to ten, place an X near the spot and phrase [see guide] that best describes you. Share your selection with the rest of the group and give reasons for placing your X where you did.**

What Happens to People Who've Never Heard of Jesus?

Short Answer: The bulk of biblical evidence suggests that people are lost without Christ, so we need to bring his message to them. After all, do *you* need Christ? Would some other way work for you? If you clearly need Christ, what makes you think people who have not heard about him don't also need Christ?

Question 1: Do you agree with the saying "Ignorance is bliss"? Why or why not?

Question 2: What do you think God's opinion is of those who are ignorant of him? Do you think he holds people morally responsible for what they don't know about him? Some people believe that as long as they don't know about the truth, they won't be held responsible for it. In that view, ignorance is an excuse that relieves people of any moral obligation to seek truth. Use these questions to get your group members to debate this issue.

Question 3: Why should missionaries be sent all over the world to expose innocent people to a knowledge that could put them at risk of hell (if they reject it)? If it were really true that ignorance implies innocence, it would be a mistake to send missionaries to expose people to a knowledge that would put them at risk. It would be a waste of the missionary's life to engage in such activity, especially if the missionary was exposed to any danger. It is interesting to note that the Bible clearly teaches that we are to go and make known the Christian message to everyone in the world, even if it requires great personal sacrifice (Ephesians 6:19–20). Why would that be necessary if people are doing fine without the gospel?

Question 4: Do you agree with the above reasoning [see guide]? Why or why not? R. C. Sproul is making the point that innocent people who are without sin don't exist— which is what the Bible also clearly teaches (see Romans

3:9–18). Everyone needs a Savior, whether they've heard about Jesus or not. He's saying the question has to be changed to "What happens to *guilty* people who have never heard of Jesus Christ?"

Question 5: **If God is completely righteous and fair in all of his judgments, do you think he will condemn people simply because they never heard the gospel? Explain.** The Bible doesn't teach that people are condemned for rejecting the Christian message; it teaches that people are condemned because they are sinners, and that rejecting the Christian message is just one more sin—not the sole act that condemns them (Ephesians 2:1–9). R. C. Sproul agrees:

> If the remote native is guilty, wherein lies his guilt? Is he punished for not believing in a Christ of whom he never heard? If God is just, that cannot be the case. If God were to punish a person for not responding to a message he had no possibility of hearing, that would be gross injustice; it would be radically inconsistent with God's own revealed justice. We can rest assured that no one is ever punished for rejecting Christ if they've never heard of him. Before we sigh too deep a breath of relief, let us keep in mind that the native is still not off the hook.... It is precisely at this point that the New Testament locates the universal guilt of man.... God's wrath is revealed not against innocence or ignorance but against ungodliness and wickedness.
>
> —*Reason to Believe*

Question 6: **What do the above verses [see guide] say about the amount of spiritual knowledge all people have, regardless of their spiritual heritage? What determines someone's eternal destiny, according to these passages?**

Question 7: **According to the above verses [see guide], what is the basis upon which God finds fault with people? Do you believe that is enough of a basis for condemnation? Why or why not?** These verses teach that all people have enough information to know that God exists and that they need him in their lives. The failure to respond to that inner prompting means they are without excuse, regardless of whether they've heard about Jesus. People who die separated from God *by their own choice* stay separated from God in eternity.

Question 8: With the above principles in mind [see guide], what conclusions can you draw so far about the destiny of those who have not heard the message of Jesus Christ? Explain.

Question 9: What other issues might be at the heart of someone's objection concerning the fate of those who've never heard of Christ?

Question 10: Do you agree with the above Straight Talk [see guide]? Why or why not?

Question 11: What is the ultimate relevancy to you personally concerning the question "What will happen to those who never hear about Jesus?" Technically speaking, these questions don't really pertain to people in your small group, because they have obviously heard about Jesus. In some cases, this question is used by people as a kind of smoke screen to avoid dealing with the claims of Christianity on a personal level. We can be certain that God is just, that no one will ever wind up in hell shaking his or her fist at God, yelling, "Unfair, unfair!" Assure those who are wondering what God is like that because of Jesus and what the Bible says, we know he is good and just, even if some aspects of these questions perplex us.

Question 12: If you believed that Jesus Christ is the only way to God, what responsibility would you feel to inform others about Jesus? You may wish to use this question to help members of your group discuss ways to reach out to others.

Question 13: Check the statement(s) below [see guide] that best describes your position at this point. Share your selection with the rest of the group and give reasons for your response.

CHAPTER SIX

Do Science and the Bible Conflict?

DISCUSSION ONE

Isn't Christianity Based on Blind Faith?

Short Answer: No, it's based on facts mixed with informed faith (not blind faith) to produce a new life in Christ.

Question 1: On the continuum below [see guide], mark the spot that best indicates how you were brought up to believe in spiritual things.

Question 2: On the continuum below [see guide], mark the spot that best indicates how you were brought up to believe in science.

Question 3: Which of the following definitions of faith [see guide] can you most relate to? Explain.

Question 4: Mark the following statements [see guide] true or false, according to your current way of thinking. Give reasons for your answers. These questions will get people talking about how their background has predisposed them to various perspectives on science and faith, including gross misconceptions about either.

Question 5: Christianity is called a faith; it is not called a science. Does this matter to you? Why or why not? What would need to change for it to be called a science? Calling Christianity a faith doesn't mean it doesn't have evidence to back it up. Lots of things aren't science but we couldn't live without them (marriage, love, parenting, even life itself). Even the great scientist Albert Einstein once said, "No, this trick won't work. . . . How on earth are you ever going to explain in terms of chemistry and physics so important a biological phenomenon as first love?" To be a science, Christianity would have to be a field of study open to repeatable experiments and theorizing about phenomena in the observable universe.

Question 6: **In your opinion, is Christianity based on fact or on faith? Explain your answer.** Christianity is based on facts, though it uses faith to activate and make personal that which facts have established. For example, salvation is based on the historical fact that Jesus died for our sins—no amount of faith can make that real if it didn't actually happen. However, once we come to know that it did happen, we receive the gift of salvation by faith (trusting God to do what he promised through Christ he would do).

Question 7: **How certain are you that your current perspective on the truth (or unreliability) of Christianity is correct? What would lead you to greater certainty about your current position? What would lead you to serious doubt about it?** Not only is it good to know we can be mistaken, it's good to know what gives us our confidence and what could erode that confidence. If a group member is closed-minded, that should come out in the response to this question.

Question 8: **What do you think of the statement "Christianity sometimes goes beyond reason but not against it"?**

Question 9: **What do you think is the role of reason in the life of a Christian? What are the limits of our powers of reasoning?** Even as great a theologian as Martin Luther said it was not wise to believe something that contradicts Scripture or reason. At his trial for heresy he said, "Reason is not our enemy, but neither is it without limits." That's why we need revelation and illumination to complete the picture of how we can gain spiritual knowledge.

Question 10: **Why do you think some people become angry when they are asked to put faith or trust in God?** Trust is essential for any relationship to work. Many people have a problem with trust, and it affects all their relationships, not just their relationship with God. Those who have difficulty trusting get upset if they're asked to trust God. The true problem is their trust issue, not the requirement to trust God.

For others, it is difficult to trust in God because he is a person so different from us—invisibility being one such difference that makes for a big problem in the relationship! But trusting is not impossible. God has provided many helps for our spiritual life (the wonders of creation, the Bible, other believers, and Jesus, to name a few).

Question 11: **Why do you think some people get angry when they are asked to give clear reasons for what they believe?** Some people don't like to have to think, because it's work. But it's important that we all know why we believe, and we are commanded in the Bible to "be prepared to give an answer to everyone who asks you to give the reason for the hope that you have" (1 Peter 3:15).

Question 12: **Do you think anyone is capable of living without some kind of faith in something? Why or why not?** Everyone has faith. Even the scientist has faith in his instruments, faith that the scientific method will give him results, faith that he will find order in the universe that makes science meaningful. The key is not to eliminate faith but to be sure your faith—in whatever area of life—has a worthy object at all times. C. S. Lewis's definition of faith, found in *Christian Reflections,* a collection of essays, may be helpful at this point: "Faith is the power of continuing to believe what we once honestly thought to be true until cogent reasons for honestly changing our minds are brought before us."

Question 13: **On a scale from one to ten, place an X near the spot and phrase [see guide] that best describes you. What reasons do you have for placing your X where you did?**

Why Are So Few Scientists Christians?

Short Answer: Currently the field of science is biased toward materialistic atheism, but that has not always been the case.

Question 1: Check the statements below [see guide] that best fit the beliefs of your growing-up years. Explain what factors shaped your opinions.

Question 2: When you were growing up, did people you knew who were scientifically inclined tend to be skeptical about spiritual matters? How about people who were spiritually minded—did they tend to be scientifically ignorant? What effect did these experiences have on the formation of your views of science and religion? Many people have had the experience of religion being forced on them at an early age. Such an approach probably damaged the credibility of Christianity, even though the fault was with a system that didn't allow for questions and with insecure teachers who wouldn't allow themselves to be questioned. Assure group members, especially the seekers in your group, that such dogmatism and narrow-mindedness is not part of your group experience, and that it isn't how biblical Christianity is supposed to be.

Question 3: Some people think science flows from facts (without any faith) and religion flows from faith (without any facts). What do you think of that distinction? This statement is a gross simplification. Scientists have a kind of faith, and religion—at least Christianity—is meaningless without facts.

Question 4: Some people think that the only way to be a Christian and a scientist at the same time is to set aside Christian beliefs so they don't color the outcome of research. What do you think of this approach? If you were a scientist, what would be your approach in trying to be objective while also believing in Jesus and the Bible?

Question 5: It is often claimed that scientists are extremely objective. Do you think this is always true? What factors besides pure facts could affect a scientist's opinions? Although it's true that as a rule scientists are encouraged to be objective, scientists have a desire to be right, and a vested interest in being right. And if they're committed to a point of view—say, nontheistic evolution—scientists may do amazing intellectual contortions to hang on to a theory. R. C. Sproul wrote about one essay he read by a well-known Nobel Prize–winning scientist. In that article the scientist argued that the idea of "spontaneous generation"—life from nonlife, with no cause—should be abandoned in science once and for all. He then proposed a new model: gradual spontaneous generation. Sproul was incredulous. "How can something gradual be spontaneous? How can something spontaneous be gradual? Our scientist wanted to debunk the myth that something can come suddenly from nothing and replace it with a better myth that something can come gradually from nothing." As Sproul noted, "Even the most astute scientists can nod. They can fall asleep at the switch and be suddenly very unscientific in their pronouncements" (R. C. Sproul, *Lifeviews*).

Consider also what the renowned atheistic scientist Carl Sagan once said: "If we must worship a power greater than ourselves, does it not make sense to revere the sun and the stars? Hidden within every astronomical investigation, sometimes so deeply buried that the researcher himself is unaware of its presence, is a kernel of awe." The apostle Paul was right on the mark: "Although they knew God, they neither glorified him as God nor gave thanks to him. . . . They exchanged the truth of God for a lie, and worshiped and served created things [in our day, Sagan revering the sun and stars] rather than the Creator" (Romans 1:21, 25).

Finally, if you think scientists are completely impartial, just attend some scientific convention or symposium—you will see plenty of ego mixed in with the facts!

Question 6: Consider the following quote by Richard Dawkins [see guide]. What do you think is the difference between being open to the possibility of a God and being open to the possible existence of fairies? The big difference between openness to God and openness to tooth fairies is the comparative amount of evidence for either. Clearly, in science, history, and human experience there is far more evidence for belief in God than for belief in tooth fairies.

Question 7: **Do you agree with the above Straight Talk [see guide] that the decision to rule out God as a possible explanation for a phenomenon is based not on science but on "unsound assumptions about reality"? Explain.** Science doesn't tell us one way or the other if the supernatural exists. If a scientist makes a statement that he doesn't believe in anything supernatural, that is a nonscientific statement. If a scientist says science can explain everything, that is a philosophical statement, not a scientific one. As J. P. Moreland observed, "Science cannot be practiced in thin air. In fact, science itself presupposes a number of substantive philosophical theses that must be assumed if science is even to get off the runway. Each of these assumptions has been challenged, and the task of stating and defending these assumptions is one of the tasks of philosophy. The conclusions of science cannot be more certain than the presuppositions they rest on and use to reach those conclusions" *(The Creation Hypothesis).*

Question 8: **Do you think it's rational to rule out, before considering the evidence, the possible involvement of God in creating the universe? Why or why not?**

Question 9: **If I carry a book across the room and then say, "Explain how the book got here," but tell you that human agency is not an option, am I being scientific? How is this example similar to or unlike ruling out God when trying to explain creation or historical events such as the resurrection of Jesus?** The resurrection of Jesus is a historical question, not a scientific one. To rule out the possible involvement of God is not a scientific act; it is a philosophical one—and a very biased one at that, because it sets aside a reasonable option before examining the evidence.

Question 10: Does scientism contain any emotional or faith elements? How is scientism different from the pure practice of science? Pure science just observes, formulates hypotheses, and tests them. Calling everything else subjective is not scientific. (Science doesn't tell you that everything except science is subjective; your philosophical bent tells you that.)

Question 11: Do you find yourself being stirred emotionally as you discuss the objectivity—or lack thereof—within the scientific community? If so, what's at the heart of your emotional response? If not, what do you think provokes people who do feel a reaction?

Question 12: What do you think explains the current prevailing attitude that brilliant thinkers couldn't possibly have objective reasons for their views about God? Some people think that to believe in God will introduce a bias in scientific inquiry. To an extent it may. But having a view of God, and knowing you have that view, is an honest way to approach a study. It is actually more objective than determining beforehand, without examining any evidence, what could not possibly be true, based on an unadmitted materialistic bias.

Question 13: What lesson could modern believers learn from this historical example [see guide]? Obviously, any attempt to distort theology to fit current "science" is doomed to look silly at some point in the future. God's revelation, even if it poses problems to modern scientific theory, is not foolishness and will ultimately be vindicated.

Question 14: On a scale from one to ten, place an X near the spot and phrase [see guide] that best describes your view. What reasons do you have for placing your X where you did?

DISCUSSION THREE

Doesn't the Big Bang Disprove a Creator?

Short Answer: No, it is actually strong evidence for a God outside of time and space who created everything—a fact many cosmologists recognize.

Question 1: From the time when you were in school, do you remember taking any course that taught things now considered outdated or even wrong? How do you think the professor would have reacted if you had known the future and could have predicted that his material would later be considered erroneous?

Question 2: What is your understanding of what the Big Bang theory is all about?

Question 3: What aspects of the Big Bang theory are generally accepted by the scientific community? What aspects are disputed? It is important for group members to state early in the discussion what they know about this theory. Some may be very well read, while others may have little or no technical knowledge. Obviously, those with less knowledge should not make dogmatic statements!

Question 4: What part of the Big Bang theory makes believers in God nervous? Why do you think that is so?

Question 5: Some have argued that the Big Bang theory actually supports belief in God, because it shows that the universe had a beginning. Do you agree? Why or why not? Along these lines, Robert Griffiths, a Heinemann recipient in mathematical physics, once joked, "If we need an atheist for a debate, I go to the philosophy department. The physics department isn't much use" (quoted by Hugh Ross in *The Creator and the Cosmos*).

Question 6: What is your reaction to the above statement by Ms. Vos Savant [see guide]? That all the galaxies were once condensed into an infinitely small point is, humanly speaking, incomprehensible, but cosmologists regularly describe that as factual. It's amazing how science can ask us to imagine such amazing "realities," yet mock religion for its "mysteries." Truly, the universe is a complex place, so simple answers to religion or science are not always forthcoming. Spiritual teachers should be respected even when they describe things difficult to grasp.

Question 7: Why do you think some people who have very little scientific training feel the need to make strong statements in areas in which they are not well qualified to speak? People are often threatened by what they don't know. Christians who feel attacked by modern science may attempt to gain easy answers in order to defend themselves or to avoid feeling stupid. A more honest approach is to admit we don't know as much as we wish we did and to do some homework in areas that interest us. Otherwise it makes sense—and seems the honest thing to do—to be quiet and listen more.

Question 8: Why do you think people get so emotional when they engage in discussions about how the universe originated?

Question 9: Do you think the Big Bang theory disproves God or his role as creator? Why or why not?

Question 10: If the universe has no creator and we are all just the dust of stars collected over billions of years, what impact does that have on how you view your life? What about how you view others?

Question 11: If we are mere globs of star dust, an accidental accumulation of molecules forged in the furnace of trillions of suns, why should we take time to discuss questions like these? If we're creatures made by a loving God, artfully assembled in his image, why should we do so? It's hard to understand why anyone would do anything other than seek his or her own well-being if we are all just a cosmic accident. "One cannot get 'ought' from 'is,' and that's what naturalism requires us to do. In short, naturalism fails to give a foundation for one of the deepest issues of human life—the issue of life and death itself. If naturalism is true, there can be no justice on the basis of an objective standard that measures all human beings. There can only be the adjudication of power: physical power, rhetorical power, political power, social power (i.e., the power of tradition) or charismatic power (i.e., the persuasive power of personality)" (James Sire, "How can I know that what I believe is true?" Mars Hill Forum).

Stepping on an ant, committing murder, and junking a car are essentially identical actions if we aren't beings created in God's image. A person's view of where we came from has enormous consequences concerning what that person does with his or her life.

Question 12: **What statement(s) below [see guide] best fits your thoughts right now? Explain your answer.**

DISCUSSION FOUR

Doesn't Evolution Contradict Genesis?

Short Answer: Yes, but evolution is probably not the best explanation for the origin of life; misinterpreting Genesis also leads to problems in explaining how life began.

Question 1: **Do you remember the first time you heard or read about the idea that humans evolved from lower forms of life? How did you react to that theory?**

Question 2: **When you were growing up, were your parents and other spiritual leaders hostile to any aspects of human evolution? If so, what reasons did they give to support their opinions?**

Question 3: **When you learned about human evolution in biology class (or another class), were you informed of any disputed areas of the theory? Cite any weaknesses or controversy you are aware of regarding the theory of evolution.** Very few people who believe in evolution can point out any weaknesses to the theory. That seems odd, because thorough study of any subject should include study of counterarguments. One professor who observed this one-sided education described a sample conversation with one of his students: "He would take it rather badly when I suggested that he was not being very scientific in his outlook if he swallowed the latest scientific dogma and, when questioned, just repeated parrot-fashion the views of the current

Archbishop of Evolution. In fact, he would be behaving like certain of those religious students he affected to despise. He would be taking on faith that he could not intellectually understand and, when questioned, would appeal to authority of a 'good book,' which in this case was *The Origin of Species*" (quoted in *Know Why You Believe* by Paul Little).

Question 4: Do you consider yourself fairly knowledgeable in the area of life sciences (biology, anthropology, biochemistry, etc.)? How does that expertise (or lack of it) affect your ability to discuss the issue of evolution with clarity and conviction? Again, listen for what level of knowledge people have about this subject. Challenge those on either side of this issue who want to make sweeping statements, reminding them that they need good facts to back up what they say.

Question 5: Do you think the account of Creation in Genesis 1 and 2 is incompatible with evolutionary theory? Why or why not?

Question 6: What is at stake for a believer in the Bible if evolution is shown to be true? What is at stake for a believer in evolution if there is a God who created life? Most people fear that if evolution is true, life was not created by God. Also, the authority of the Bible is questioned; clearly, whoever wrote Genesis 1 and 2 had no idea what they were talking about. If the story of Creation is just a made-up fable, what else in the Bible also could be made up? On the other side, if God did create us, a believer in evolution will have to modify his or her belief system, which up to now has assumed we're an accident caused by chance.

Question 7: What evidence are you aware of that shows life is the product of intelligent design rather than random, naturalistic forces? Norman Geisler, in the article "*Darwin's Black Box:* A Brief Review," writes,

> The most recent and hottest attack on Darwinism comes from Michael Behe, Associate Professor of Biochemistry

at Lehigh University in *Darwin's Black Box,* NY: The Free Press, 1996.

The thesis of the book is very simple: 1) Irreducible complexity cannot be accounted for by small incremental changes; 2) Life, especially on the molecular level, is often irreducibly complex; 3) Therefore, Darwinism has no explanation for such life.

Further, 1) Irreducible complexity is best accounted for by intelligent design; 2) Such irreducible complexity exists in living cells; 3) Hence, the best explanation for such life is an intelligent Designer.

Darwin admitted: "If it could be demonstrated that any complex organ existed which could not possibly have been formed by numerous, successive, slight modifications, my theory would absolutely break down" (Darwin, *Origin of Species*).

Evolutionist Richard Dawkins agrees: "Evolution is very possibly not, in actual fact, always gradual. But it must be gradual when it is being used to explain the coming into existence of complicated, apparently designed objects, like eyes. For if it is not gradual in these cases, it ceases to have any explanatory power at all. Without gradualness in these cases, we are back to miracle, which is a synonym for the total absence of [naturalistic] explanation" (Dawkins, *River Out of Eden*).

Michael Behe challenges: "No one at Harvard University, no one at the National Institutes of Health, no member of the National Academy of Sciences, no Nobel Prize winner—no one at all can give a detailed account of how the cilium, or vision, or blood clotting, or any complex biochemical process might have developed in a Darwinian fashion. But we are here. All these things got here somehow; if not in a Darwinian fashion, then how?" (Behe, *Darwin's Black Box*).

Question 8: **What is your reaction to the claim that Genesis contains poetic elements? What is your reaction to the claim that it teaches we were created and didn't randomly evolve?** This question may generate some heated discussion because it strikes close to home for believers who have a high view of Scripture. Some interpreters are extremely uncomfortable with taking any statements in Genesis poetically; for them, if Genesis says there was "evening and morning," then there were twenty-four hours and there was an evening and a morning (even though the sun was yet to be created!). Our view is that Genesis is an accurate description of the creation of the universe and of life but leaves out many details that would interest a scientist. It only makes sense that God would describe how he made the world and us in terms that any culture or education level could understand. He knew getting bogged down in scientific precision would lose multitudes of readers with no access to that knowledge, so he revealed his work in broad strokes so we'd all be clear about the "who" and "what" but not necessarily the "how."

Question 9: What emotions stir in you as you discuss the issue of evolution versus creation?

Question 10: Do you think it's possible to be completely objective when discussing evolution versus creation? Why or why not?

Question 11: What emotion do you suppose an atheistic scientist feels when encountering evidence of a creator? What emotion does a believer feel upon finding explanations for phenomena that don't require God's involvement? Someone committed to rejecting God must be terrified when evidence for his existence emerges! Likewise, a believer is probably frightened when it appears his or her belief is unfounded. No one likes to be wrong; no one wants to look foolish. This is especially true when it comes to such monumental beliefs as where we came from and who made us.

Question 12: On a scale from one to ten, place an X near the spot and phrase [see guide] that best describes you. What reasons do you have for placing your X where you did?

If the Bible Is True,
Why Isn't It More Scientific?

Short Answer: The Bible is aimed at all societies and all education levels, so it uses the language of observation rather than precise scientific terminology. Besides, science changes so rapidly that any scientific description would be outdated in a few years, making the Bible sound silly.

Question 1: Did your early spiritual teachers lead you to accept the Bible without question? What rationale were you offered for their certainty (or skepticism)?

Question 2: What is your current level of confidence in the reliability of the Bible when it touches on matters of history or science? Some people make a split between relying on the Bible for spiritual truth and believing what it says about "secular" issues—history, for example. Such a split is not honest, however, because spiritual truth and history are inextricably intertwined. God revealed himself in history, and Jesus was a man of history who provided for salvation at a point in history. Our faith is invalid if the Bible's historical claims are erroneous. Besides, why would you trust a source for truths you couldn't prove (spiritual ones), when you found it was corrupt in other areas where you could test it (such as history)?

Question 3: If the Bible can be shown, through the science of archaeology, to be reliable in matters of history, would that affect your level of trust in it regarding other areas? Would you still trust the Bible if it taught things known to be historically or scientifically untrue?

Question 4: What do you think of the above comparisons [see guide]?

Question 5: If archaeology ever did find an artifact that contradicted the Bible, what would that do to your faith? **Explain.** It may not totally destroy a person's faith to discover an archaeological contradiction, because it is always possible that we haven't understood correctly what the archaeological find means. Still, to be consistent, we would have to grant that a known contradiction between the Bible and archaeology would effectively erode our faith in the Bible as reliable and as a source of truth from God.

Question 6: **Although the Bible is undeniably a prescientific book, do you think it teaches belief in outright errors? Why or why not?**

Question 7: **What is the difference between being imprecise and being in error? Do you think the Bible's descriptive language negates its reliability as a source for absolute truth? Explain.** Estimates can be false if they are way off. But they're not false if they're estimates and taken as such. Language that is not precise can be right or wrong, but it is not automatically wrong just because it's imprecise. God gives us lots of pictures of how much he loves us—is it a problem that he does so without mathematical precision?

Question 8: **What do you think about the enduring quality of the Bible, considering it's more than twenty centuries old and has been ruthlessly criticized by skeptics?**

Question 9: **Why do you think some people seem to enjoy finding "contradictions" in the Bible?** If a person has an ax to grind, finding so-called contradictions can be one way to get back at the religion or religious person who made him or her angry. That person needs to be more honest about what is gong on and to stop attacking the Bible when something else is the real issue.

Question 10: **Do you think this analogy [see guide] adequately explains why the Bible, though it claims to come from an omniscient God, is in common, everyday language—without scientific precision? Why or why not?** The theological term used to describe this is "to condescend," and it is a good way to picture what God has to do to speak to us on our finite, limited level. He must get truth down to us on our level, and by taking on our form of communication, he will necessarily be constrained by its limitations.

The amazing thing is how well his revelation does work, in spite of the limits of language. And of course, by sending the Word incarnate, he has made himself very clear: "In the past God spoke to our forefathers through the prophets at many times and in various ways, but in these last days he has spoken to us by his Son, whom he appointed heir of all things, and through whom he made the universe. The Son is the radiance of God's glory and the exact representation of his being" (Hebrews 1:1–3).

Question 11: Check the statement(s) below [see guide] that best reflects your opinion. What reasons do you have for choosing that statement(s)?

DISCUSSION SIX

Won't Scientific Progress Make God Unnecessary?

Short Answer: No, because science has its limits, and belief in God isn't based on the observations of science. The evidence for God is positive; he's not just the explanation for things science doesn't know yet.

Question 1: Describe a time when you had to drastically revise your view of God. What emotions came with that change?

Question 2: Why do you think people have such optimism about the possibility that science will answer all our questions and solve all our problems? It's easy to be impressed with advances in science, because they are so startling and beneficial. But when we look at the human condition, at war and oppression and dysfunction everywhere we turn, optimism about science solving all our problems seems far too idealistic.

Question 3: What do you think of the following statement: "If we use God to explain what we cannot understand, God shrinks every time we learn something new"?

Question 4: Will your god (if you believe in one) ever be "killed by a whiff of science or a dose of common sense"? Why or why not?

Question 5: The "God of the gaps" fallacy says we use God to explain what science can't—we fill in the gaps of our knowledge with an appeal to the activity of God. Do you think that is the case with Christian theism? Explain. Our belief in God will not hold up to scrutiny if it is based merely on what we can't explain with science. Jesus gives us positive evidence to help us believe in God, so we won't fall into the trap of basing our theism merely on the absence of a reasonable alternative to a scientific theory.

Question 6: Many areas of life (such as the act of falling in love) are not subject to empirical scientific testing or even to being improved through science. Despite this limitation of science, the notion persists that scientific knowledge will eventually do away with belief in God. Do you agree? Why or why not?

Question 7: How has science strengthened your belief in God, if you are a believer? If you aren't a believer, what has science taught you that makes belief in God seem unreasonable?

Question 8: What tough question(s) about some scientific issue still troubles you? Although this guide (and series) comes to a close on this issue with this session, as the leader, you should pay attention to what people in your group, especially seekers, say here. At a minimum it would help to have follow-up conversations about these topics, and it may make sense to have the whole group explore some of the issues together.

Question 9: Do you agree that something outside the universe is required to explain the universe sufficiently? Why or why not?

Question 10: If you were to abandon all belief in God, what unsettling questions come to mind? C. S. Lewis, a former atheist turned believer, pointed out that just as the Christian has his moments when the clamor of this visible and audible world is so persistent and the whisper of the spiritual world so faint that faith and reason can hardly stick to their guns, so, as I well remember, the atheist too has his moments of shuddering misgiving, of an all but irresistible suspicion that old tales may after all be true, that something or someone from outside may at any moment break into his neat, explicable, mechanical universe. Believe in God and you will have to face hours when it seems obvious that this material world is the only reality; disbelieve in Him and you must face hours when this material world seems to shout at you that it is not all.

—"Religion: Reality or Substitute?"
in *Christian Reflections*

Question 11: **Can you imagine a discovery of science that would destroy your belief in God? Explain.**

Question 12: **On a scale from one to ten, place an *X* near the spot and phrase [see guide] that best describes your opinion. What reasons do you have for placing your *X* where you did?**

CHAPTER SEVEN

Why Become a Christian?

DISCUSSION ONE

Why Would Anyone Think I'm Not a Christian?

Short Answer: Contrary to popular belief, being a Christian is not a matter of religious performance; it is a matter of a new spiritual birth—being "born again."

Question 1: Describe an occasion when you (or someone you know) believed you had the necessary ticket to attend a special event but for some reason were denied entry.

Question 2: If you were to identify someone as a Christian, what definitive factors or reasons would you look for to support that claim? Be careful to resist the temptation to correct your group members' responses at this point. Remember, this is a discovery process for seekers. Let them feel your acceptance no matter how they answer these questions.

Question 3: Which of the activities in the following list [see guide] qualifies someone to be a Christian? Check all that apply and give reasons for your answer(s). None of the activities listed (including being born into a Christian family) qualifies a person to be a Christian. Those activities are things that most likely would be part of a Christian's lifestyle *as a result of* receiving Jesus as forgiver and leader, but none of them are what makes a person a Christian. One crosses the line to become a Christian by receiving Jesus as the forgiver of one's sins and new leader of one's life.

Question 4: **What role do you think religious activity plays in being a true Christian?**

Question 5: **Do you think it is possible to have a false sense of security about being a Christian? If you answered yes, name some examples of false hopes. If no, why do you think a person can't be wrong about his or her claim to be a Christian?** It is certainly possible to have a false sense of security about being a Christian. The Bible abounds with warnings against spiritual presumption (see next Straight Talk). Some people in your group may define being a Christian differently than the Bible does. Those people may still be Christians (despite their erroneous definitions), but they need to know the truth about what it means to be a Christ follower. And of course, some in your group may think they are believers but are not. The tough questions posed in this session are so important because people's eternal destinies are at stake.

Question 6: **The people referenced in the above verses [see guide] were definitely busy doing religious things. What do you think is the difference between an actively religious person who enters the kingdom of heaven and an actively religious person who does not?** The key to this question is Jesus' phrase "I never knew you." To *know* someone in the biblical sense is to have an intimate relationship. Of course, being omniscient, Jesus knows everyone and he knows everything about everyone. But he doesn't *know* the people in these verses personally, because they have rejected a relationship with him. Jesus refuses to acknowledge those who, in spite of associating with spiritual activities and spiritually minded people, don't have a true connection—a personal relationship—with him. So regardless of what these people do, there is no spiritual life or salvation present in them, and therefore they are still lost in sin.

Question 7: **What is the correlation between initially *becoming* a Christian and *living out* one's life as a Christian?**

A true Christian is one who at some point has accepted Jesus Christ as the only way to be forgiven for sin. As a result of receiving that tremendous gift, a Christian places his or her life gratefully into God's hands. That gratitude is expressed in a variety of ways, among them: worship, development of godly character, service, fellowship with other Christians, spiritual growth, sharing one's faith, and honoring God in every area of life.

Question 8: **Do you think a person, to be a true Christian, must be born into the Christian religion, or could he or she be converted into it, or both? Explain your answer.** No one is ever born a Christian. Everyone must make his or her own personal decision about how to respond to Christ's offer of forgiveness. (See comments in next question.)

Question 9: **What do you think it means to be born again?** The term "born again" is another way of communicating that a person has to *choose* to become a Christian—not *ooze* his or her way in. It implies that accepting Christ is a beginning, a spiritual rebirth of a whole new life in Christ (2 Corinthians 5:17). John R. W. Stott, in his book *Basic Christianity,* puts it this way: "Whatever his parentage and upbringing, every responsible adult is obliged to make up his own mind for or against Christ. We cannot remain neutral. Nor can we drift into Christianity. Nor can anyone else settle the matter for us. We must decide for ourselves."

Question 10: **What's the difference between being religious and being born again? Why would Jesus tell someone like Nicodemus, who was already very religious, to be born again?** A religious person is not necessarily a true Christian. Nicodemus apparently counted on his religiosity (adherence to spiritual traditions and rituals), and Jesus warned him that to do so was to make a false assumption. Religious people tend to take their stand on their heritage, and Jesus made it clear that the only way for us to understand and know God is to consider our "religiousness" worthless and begin to think in terms of starting all over again.

The apostle Paul realized he needed to be born again in spite of his religious heritage. He wrote of himself,

> If anyone else thinks he has reasons to put confidence in the flesh, I have more: circumcised on the eighth day, of the people of Israel, of the tribe of Benjamin, a Hebrew of Hebrews; in regard to the law, a Pharisee; as for zeal, persecuting the church; as for legalistic righteousness, faultless. But whatever was to my profit I now consider loss for the sake of Christ. What is more, I consider everything a loss compared to the surpassing greatness of knowing Christ Jesus my Lord, for whose sake I have lost all things. I consider them rubbish, that I may gain Christ and be found in him, not having a righteousness of my own that comes from the law, but that which is through faith in Christ—the righteousness that comes from God and is by faith.
>
> —Philippians 3:4–9

Question 11: **In what ways are you similar to Nicodemus? How are you different?**

Question 12: **If you were to encounter Jesus today, would he tell you there's still something missing in your life? Why or why not?** Please use these last two questions to assist your group members to take a hard look at their own lives to see where they personally stand with Jesus Christ. Be sensitive that they may each be at different places and may need your individual counsel to help determine their next steps.

Question 13: **Why does talking about being born again often create negative images and angry reactions?**

Question 14: **Check the statement(s) below [see guide] that best describes your position at this point. Share your selection with the rest of the group and give reasons for your response.** Pay special attention to the responses your group members give here, so you will know specific issues to address when you meet with individuals outside the group.

DISCUSSION TWO

What's the Big Deal About Sin?

Short Answer: Dismissing sin as irrelevant or without consequence is spiritually fatal.

Question 1: **Do you think Christianity dwells too much on the negative, because of its apparent emphasis on sin, hell, and judgment? Explain your answer.** While it may be true that some believers are negative people who cloak their irascibility with spiritual language, it's hard to imagine how lovingly warning people of the eternal consequence of their rebellion against God could be considered too negative. Nonetheless, this is a widely held opinion.

Question 2: **According to your understanding of the Bible, what separates people from God: a propensity to sin, a lack of knowledge about God, or both? Explain your answer.** The central human dilemma is spiritual rebellion against God, not ignorance of him. Because of God's revelation of himself through creation and conscience, we have more knowledge of him than we might think—enough to make us "without excuse" (Romans 1:18–20; 2:12–16).

Question 3: **Do you believe that people are, for the most part, basically good, basically bad, or somewhere in between? Explain.** As the next Straight Talk points out, the Bible clearly teaches that not one person is without sin and in fact we are all born into sin. Therefore no one is "basically good." Everyone has a sin problem.

Question 4: **How would you define sin? What are the repercussions of sin, if any?** Sin is any disobedience against God—any failure to "hit the mark" of his perfect standard, whether that be active rebellion or passive indifference. Sin is the desire to turn away from God in any area of life and leave him out of the matter. The repercussions of sin are the immediate loss of God's presence and guidance (spiritual death), and that same loss forever (eternal death, or what the Bible calls "the second death" [Revelation 20:6, 14]).

Question 5: How do you respond to the biblical claim above [see guide] that the sin in your life is so offensive to God that it has spiritually separated you from him?

Question 6: The Bible also teaches that the penalty of sin is spiritual death. What do you suppose it means to be spiritually dead? To be spiritually dead means to exist without connection to God and to be under his judgment. It means being without access to the kingdom of God. It is possible to be very much alive physically and yet dead spiritually. Physical death, in this case, would put an end to having any access to God's physical world.

Question 7: Do you think it is possible to be indifferent or neutral toward God without necessarily being antagonistic or hostile toward him? Why or why not? See comments for question 8 below.

Question 8: How might people who appear to be indifferent or neutral toward God really be his enemies? According to the Bible, the very act of being indifferent or neutral toward God is a way of telling him you are your own god. If you lived in a kingdom and the king asked if you were one of his citizens and you replied that you weren't committed one way or the other, he would undoubtedly question you until you declared where your loyalties lay. Your "neutrality" could well be considered treason, especially if you were taking advantage of the benefits of the king's kingdom without any commitment to it. To live in God's world yet assert that the King has no say over your affairs—even if you haven't declared yourself at war with him—leaves you guilty of the same offense.

By virtue of God's greatness and lordship over all of his creation, he deserves our complete devotion and submission to his leadership. Failure to give it—even though open revolt hasn't been voiced—denies him that position and greatly offends him.

Question 9: In what sense is God the one seeking us first, before we seek him? Because God initiated a costly plan to redeem all of us who were separated from him, we know that it is he who greatly longs for us to come back to him—much more than we want him. In addition, by sending us prophets, his written Word, and his own Son, and by prodding every one of us through the convicting ministry of the Holy Spirit (John 16:7–8), he is clearly the original "seeker."

Question 10: **How does the above illustration [see guide] demonstrate that when it comes to our shortcomings before God, comparing ourselves with others seems foolish?** All of us can find at least one person who makes us feel superior. But the standard by which we measure ourselves needs to be Jesus Christ himself.

Question 11: **Some say God rates people using a scale. He places all the good things you've done on one side of that scale, and the bad stuff on the other. Whichever side outweighs the other determines whether you are a good person or a bad person. Do you agree with this analogy? Why or why not? Evaluate the pros and cons of this rating system.** No amount of good we can muster can make up for the loss incurred by sin. It's like telling someone dying of two punctured lungs to get better by breathing harder or faster. It might do some good for a short while, but it won't heal the wound or save the person's life.

Question 12: **Does it feel negative or scary to admit that you may have a sin problem? Why or why not?** Once a person honestly comes to grips with personal sin, there should be a deep sense of regret and sorrow at the realization of the blatant insult that sin is to God. We should want to resolve the situation—and do it *God's* way—as soon as possible. Healthy fear can lead to accepting God's grace and love, which in turn provides great peace and hope for the future (2 Corinthians 7:10).

Question 13: **Do you have a tendency to minimize or maximize your sin by comparing yourself with others? Explain.**

Question 14: **How have you or will you deal with the sin problem that the Bible claims all of us have?** Use the answers to this question to follow up with members in your group on an individual basis. What an exciting thing it would be to assist someone in your group to realize he or she needs and wants Jesus Christ to provide forgiveness and new life! There's no greater privilege than to be used by God to help someone cross the line and invite Jesus into his or her life.

Question 15: Check the statement(s) below [see guide] that best describes your position at this point. Share your selection with the rest of the group and give reasons for your response.

DISCUSSION THREE

Why Can't I Make It on My Own?

Short Answer: Because no one has what it takes; God expects moral perfection, and any sin—only one—makes that forever impossible.

Question 1: Describe a situation in which you or someone you know stubbornly refused to accept the help of another person. What is it about human nature that causes us to refuse assistance?

Question 2: Suppose you spent several thousand dollars to purchase a car for a close friend who was in desperate need of one. How would you react if, after you offered your gift with no strings attached, your friend refused the "gift" and instead insisted on paying you fifty dollars for it? When we give a free gift, we get joy out of seeing someone receive and enjoy that gift. But if they offer to make payment for that gift—especially if what they offer is paltry compared with what the gift is really worth—the offer can feel like an insult. Considering that Jesus paid for salvation with his blood, how ridiculous is it for us to think we can offer God our "good works" as payment? How close do our attempts at goodness come to what his perfect and pure life was worth?

Question 3: According to the verses listed above [see guide], what is God's provision for solving the sin problem of the human race? God provided his Son, an innocent lamb without blemish or defect, as the perfect and only worthy sacrifice able to make complete and total payment for the sins of the world. Cliffe Knechtle summarizes things this way: "God is just, holy and morally perfect. We all stand guilty before God because we fall far short of his perfection. But the Bible also reveals that God is loving and merciful. He has provided a way to escape the condemnation we deserve. He has sent his Son to die for us" (*Give Me An Answer*, 3a).

Question 4: **How does the statement "People are more likely to ignore 'doctor's orders' when they are unwilling to admit they are really sick" relate to our attitude toward solving the sin problem God's way?** Some people believe they have no sin problem, and as a result see no need for forgiveness. Jesus said he came to call on those who are sick, not on those who are well. To change the analogy slightly, in reality we're all blind, but as soon as we think we have sight, we stop looking for a cure—and remain spiritually blind. (Jesus said this very thing to the Pharisees in John 9:40–41.)

Question 5: **What are the various ways in which people insist on earning forgiveness or attempt to fix the sin problem by their own efforts?**

Question 6: **Why do you think people strive to solve the sin problem in their own way instead of doing it God's way?** The two biggest reasons are pride and disbelief. Pride says, "I can do it myself; I don't need your help. I don't want to have to be indebted to you, God." Disbelief says, "I know Jesus said he paid it all, but I can't believe it's that easy. There must be a catch, so I'll take precautions rather than trust his promises."

Question 7: **What's the difference between a gift and a wage? According to the Bible, is salvation from the penalty of sin a wage or a gift? Give a reason for your answer.** A wage is something you earn and is due you. A gift is something someone gives you that is not tied to performance in any way but nonetheless *must* be received by you to become yours.

Question 8: What is your reaction to the Christian teaching that says it is absolutely impossible to do anything whatsoever to save yourself from the penalty of sin?

Question 9: How difficult is it for you to admit that you cannot, on your own, bridge the gap between you and God caused by your sin?

Question 10: Looking back on your life, what obstacles may have made it difficult for you to trust God? Is trusting God for your destiny easy or difficult for you now? Why?

Question 11: In what ways might you expect a person to respond after receiving God's free offer of total and complete forgiveness? How would (or did) you react? The previous three or four questions are designed to help you, as the leader, discern where your group members are in their spiritual journeys. Please pay special attention to indications your group members may give concerning their readiness to personally accept Jesus Christ as forgiver and leader. Of course, the decision to receive Christ must not be coerced in any way, but when the time is right, you may wish to invite members to do this through prayer—even during the session if it seems appropriate.

Question 12: Check the statement(s) below [see guide] that best describes your position at this point. Share your selection with the rest of the group and give reasons for your response.

DISCUSSION FOUR

Why Is Jesus So Important?

Short Answer: Jesus, God's Son, is the *only* one able to forgive our sins, because he alone paid the price: his life in exchange for ours.

Question 1: Describe a time when you needed to get through to someone in charge, only to be put on hold, transferred, or even disconnected. How did this make you feel?

Question 2: Do you think it is possible to go directly to God without first having to go through Jesus as a mediator? **Explain.** Of course God is omniscient and hears our prayers—in that sense we don't need to go through Jesus to get to God. (Satan directly goes to God in this sense—see Job 1:6.) But God sees our sin and therefore cannot have *fellowship* with us. It is only when Christ takes away the guilt and substitutes his righteousness in us that God can connect with us and have a close relationship.

Question 3: What are some of the benefits the world has gained as a result of Jesus Christ's life and teaching ministry?

Question 4: What do you think was Jesus Christ's ultimate reason for coming to this world? Answers will probably vary. Let them all stand for now, because the Straight Talk that follows will help make this more clear.

Question 5: Jesus' death was more than a tragedy; it was intentional. What was the purpose of Jesus' death? How exactly was that purpose fulfilled by his death on the cross?

Question 6: What reasons do you think Christianity gives for its assertion that Jesus is the only way to God?

Question 7: What is it about Jesus that, according to the Bible, enabled him to become the only worthy payment for sin and therefore the only possible bridge between God and all humankind? Refer to the Straight Talk "Jesus Paid the Price" for some helpful commentary for the last three questions.

Question 8: According to the above verses [see guide], what choice did Jesus have in laying down his life for us? How does your answer impact you?

Question 9: In what ways can you relate to the struggle Jesus faced in following the will of the Father? Describe a time when you chose to do the right thing even though it was a personal sacrifice for you.

Question 10: **In what ways is Jesus' life, death, and resurrection an example to you of how to live your life?** Because Jesus was fully human, he wrestled with the choice to give up his life as a sacrifice on our behalf. He loved and trusted the Father, and he loved those his death would save. But the pain and spiritual torment of taking upon himself the sins of the world was nonetheless real—and agonizing. This struggle can be an example for us, by showing us we need to do the right thing even when it's hard to do so. It can also be a comfort to know that just because we've decided something is right, it doesn't mean it will be easy (Hebrews 21:1–4).

Question 11: **Why is Jesus' resurrection proof of his ability to keep his promises?** The Resurrection is proof that Jesus is no ordinary man. In all of history—among all other religious leaders—it establishes him as the supreme source of truth. It is proof that our sin did not overwhelm him but is forgivable, because he overcame sin's penalty through coming back to life. As Paul Little *(Know What You Believe)* explains, "The implications of the Resurrection are enormous. We should understand them as fully as possible—and *enjoy* them. The Resurrection fully confirms the truth and value of what Jesus taught and did. . . . Because of the Resurrection, we know we are not trusting in a myth; we know that our sins are actually forgiven through the death of Christ. Certainty and forgiveness are based on the empty tomb! Christ is the only One who has ever come back from death to tell men about the beyond. In *His* words we know we have the authoritative Word of God Himself."

Question 12: **What difference does it make to you personally that Jesus Christ came into the world, lived a perfect life, died on the cross for your sins, and rose again?**

Question 13: **Check the statement(s) below [see guide] that best describes your position at this point. Share your selection with the rest of the group and give reasons for your response.**

Can Someone Like Me Really Change?

Short Answer: Yes, because God provides his followers with new life and a new source of power through the Holy Spirit so even *you* can change!

Question 1: Describe a time when you felt overwhelmed by a project at work or school. Did the pressure drive you to work harder or were you paralyzed by it? How did you cope with the stress?

Question 2: What aspect of living the Christian life seems overwhelming or too difficult to you?

Question 3: What do you think is behind the obligation people feel to clean up their act before they can become a Christian? It is common for people to think that God will not accept them until they somehow first straighten up their lives. It is a humbling thing to openly come to God, claiming no worthiness of our own. The truth is that God *has* accepted us already; all we have to do is come. Any attempt to clean up our act first is really an effort to save ourselves—and that is something we could never do. The only way we can ever come to him is just as we are with flaws and all. At that point, meeting us right where we're at, Jesus forgives and cleanses us.

Question 4: What sorts of things do you think a person needs to do before becoming a Christian? The *only* thing a person needs to do to become a Christian is simply accept the free gift God offers in his Son. To do that you must: (1) *admit* you're a sinner in need of forgiveness; (2) *be willing* to turn away from sin and cooperate with God to make changes; (3) *believe* that Jesus completed the work of salvation through his death and resurrection; and (4) personally *receive* Jesus Christ as forgiver and leader. The great scholar F. F. Bruce *(Paul: Apostle of the Heart Set Free)* agrees:

> If there is to be any salvation for [anyone], then, it must be based not on ethical achievement but on the grace of God.

What [all people] need alike, in fact, is to have their records blotted out by an act of divine amnesty and to have the assurance of acceptance by God for no merit of their own but by his spontaneous mercy. For this need God has made provision in Christ. Thanks to his redemptive work, men may find themselves 'in the clear' before God. . . . The benefits of the atonement thus procured may be appropriated by faith—and only by faith. . . . True [Christianity] is not a matter of rules and regulations. God does not deal with people like an accountant, but accepts them freely when they respond to his love, and implants the Spirit of Christ in their hearts so that they may show to others the love they have received from him.

Question 5: **If salvation is not a matter of self-improvement, on what basis was this promise [see guide] made? How does this precedent give you hope?** The promise of salvation was based entirely on what God does, not on what the person does. That precedent means we too can have a relationship with God based on his perfection, not ours.

Question 6: **Have you ever felt defeated by the feeling that the standards of the Christian life are too hard to measure up to? Why or why not?** Think about when two people plan to be married. It means some radical changes are coming—involving a whole new way of living. In a similar way, receiving Christ means being willing to live life differently— now Christ is the leader, and honoring him needs to take top priority. As Paul Little warns, this is a stumbling block for some:

We need to be reminded that ultimately man's basic problem is not intellectual; it is moral. Once in a while our answer won't satisfy someone. His rejection of the answer doesn't invalidate it. On the other hand, he may be convinced and still not become a Christian. I've had fellows tell me, "You've answered every one of my questions to my satisfaction." After thanking them for the flattery, I've asked, "Are you going to become a Christian then?" And they've smiled a little sheepishly, "Well, no." "Why not?"

I've inquired. "Frankly, it would mean too radical a change in my way of life." Many people are not prepared to let anyone else, including God, run their lives. It's not that they can't believe; but they won't believe.

—How to Give Away Your Faith

Question 7: **Do you agree with the quote by John Hick in the above Straight Talk [see guide]? Why or why not? Have you ever known of someone who truly lived the Christian life? What do you think enabled him or her to live as a Christian should?**

Question 8: **In what ways is the Christian life impossible to live? In what ways do you think Jesus Christ makes the Christian life possible to live?** Because of our sin, no matter how hard we try, we will always fall short. In this sense we can never copy the perfect life Jesus lived, though we might want to. But when Jesus comes into our lives, he begins to do a work in us. Changes start to occur. He gives us the Holy Spirit to guide us and bring us new convictions. He puts new desires and goals in our hearts. By dwelling in us, he gives us the motivation and strength and power to live a Christ-honoring life.

Question 9: **How and when does the change a person experiences in becoming a Christian start to happen?**

Question 10: **What role does God play in changing people? Would you describe yourself as a person changed by God? Explain.** The change begins the moment a person receives Christ into his or her life. It may be a very gradual change, but God begins his work immediately. He continues to grow us up in our newfound faith; our responsibility is to follow him on a daily basis.

Question 11: **Would it be intimidating or frightening to you to be known as a committed Christian? Why or why not?**

Question 12: **Do you ever feel that you cannot change enough to live as a Christian? Explain.**

Question 13: According to the verses in the previous Straight Talk [see guide], to what extent does God commit himself to you and to the changes that occur in you? How does this make you feel?

Question 14: On a scale from one to ten, place an *X* near the spot and phrase [see guide] that best describes you. Share your selection with the rest of the group and give reasons for placing your *X* where you did.

DISCUSSION SIX

How Does Someone Actually Become a Christian?

Short Answer: By receiving Jesus Christ: his provision for sin, his power for living, and his indwelling presence forever. His offer of forgiveness and new life is open to any and all who will ask for it. The only thing one needs to do to become a Christian is simply accept the free gift God offers in his Son. To do that you must: (1) *admit* you're a sinner in need of forgiveness; (2) *be willing* to turn away from sin and cooperate with God to make changes; (3) *believe* that Jesus completed the work of salvation through his death and resurrection; and (4) personally *receive* Jesus Christ as forgiver and leader.

Question 1: When you first heard about Christianity, what did you think was its message? How would you summarize that message now, to the best of your understanding?

Question 2: Do you think becoming a Christian is an ongoing process, something that happens at a specific point in time, or a combination of the two? Give reasons for your answer. Becoming a Christian is a combination of an ongoing process of discovery and conviction and a point-in-time conversion. The specifics of each person's journey vary, but Jesus himself said you cannot see the kingdom of God without being born again. Even though a person may not remember a specific point in time when he or she received

Christ, Jesus comes in only by invitation. So if Christ is there, he was invited.

Question 3: **If salvation is a free gift, isn't it automatically applied to everyone—even atheists? Why or why not?** God will not force salvation upon anyone; to do so would be out of character for him. Instead he provides salvation as a gift. He wants people to freely choose a relationship with him, so salvation is not a coercive act but an offer made and received. If God gave salvation to those who didn't want it, he would be abrogating their power of choice. That would be a violation of the human dignity he gave to all by virtue of making creatures in his image.

Question 4: **Do you agree or disagree with the above analogy [see guide]? Explain. What stage are you in right now: the "getting to know you" stage, the "ready to make a commitment" stage, or the "I've already said 'I do'" stage? Why do you think becoming a Christian requires an intentional response?** Becoming a Christian requires an intentional response because God values our power of choice and wants to honor his commitment to invest us with autonomy. An unopened present can never benefit the recipient; salvation not accepted is ineffectual. A response to God is the very essence of having a relationship with him, and a relationship is possible only when the wills of both parties are respected. If only one party's will is honored, it's called slavery.

Question 5: **What is the difference between an intellectual assent to a set of beliefs and an actual acceptance of those same beliefs?** In the study guide *Friendship with God* (Walking with God series), Don Cousins and Judson Poling write, "At its core, Christianity is Christ. Christians embrace a person, not merely a philosophy. It is not knowing about his teaching so much as it is knowing him. The greatest misunderstanding about Christianity today, even in the church, is the perception that God's bottom-line requirements are deeds to be done and beliefs to be believed. The Christ who spoke is bypassed for the things he spoke; the Guide is left behind for the guidance; the Commander is ignored in the carrying out of the commands."

Question 6: **What does it mean to "receive" Jesus? How is *receiving* a gift different from *earning* it?** Receiving Jesus means to invite him into your life so he comes to dwell in you, and all the benefits of his life become yours (John 1:12; 5:24; 1 Peter 2:24; Revelation 3:20). Receiving a gift is not the same as earning it. Our part in the transaction is to acknowledge and accept the gift; God's part is to apply it to us upon our decision to receive it.

Question 7: **According to these verses [see guide], what do we need to do to receive eternal life? What does God do?**

Question 8: **Some people think of salvation as preparing for a quiz. They think the important thing is to learn the right answer to the question, asked by God, "Why should I let you into heaven?" Why do you think this misses the point of what God wants from a relationship with us?** God doesn't want a universe full of people with right answers; he wants children who love him. He didn't die to prepare us for some heavenly entrance exam; he died to bring us life—to make possible an eternity of relating together.

Question 9: **What light does this [see guide] shed on the true meaning of eternal life and on God's intention for our relationship with him?** If correct theology saves you, Satan is a saint—his theology is flawless (James 2:19). Obviously, incorrect theology is no virtue. But if people gather knowledge, thinking they are getting closer to God or earning favor in his sight, they are mistaken. Knowledge of God in the biblical sense is not accumulation of information; it is knowledge in the sense of intimacy. God wants to know us deeply and enjoy the closest possible spiritual connection with us.

Question 10: **Does any obstacle prevent you from crossing that line, once and for all, and embracing God's forgiveness and leadership? Explain your answer.**

Question 11: Does anything keep you from declaring the resurrected Jesus as the forgiver and leader of your life? If you're comfortable doing so, tell the group where you are with this decision. If there is anything holding you back, share that as well. These last two questions are really the bottom line of this session, and perhaps of the entire Tough Questions series. Our desire is that as people are stretched and challenged to express where they are in their spiritual journey, they will eventually come to the point where they will open their lives to the saving work of Christ and cross that line into his kingdom. Please help the members of your group honestly assess what holds them back from making the most important and rewarding decision of their lives. Be in prayer as you gently challenge each person to accept God's wonderful offer of love and forgiveness.

Question 12: What's your reaction to the word of encouragement offered in the Straight Talk above [see guide]? What to you would feel like the right thing to do at this point in this series of studies? Where would you like to go from here?

Question 13: If you could ask God one question you knew he would answer right away, what would it be? Use these last two questions as a springboard for deciding what your group will do after the completion of this guide.

Question 14: On a scale from one to ten, place an *X* near the spot and phrase [see guide] that best describes you. Share your selection with the rest of the group and give reasons for placing your *X* where you did.

Willow Creek Association
Vision, Training, Resources for Prevailing Churches

This resource was created to serve you and to help you in building a local church that prevails!
Since 1992, the Willow Creek Association (WCA) has been linking like-minded, action-oriented churches with each other and with strategic vision, training, and resources. Now a worldwide network of over 6,400 churches from more than ninety denominations, the WCA works to equip Member Churches and others with the tools needed to build prevailing churches. Our desire is to inspire, equip, and encourage Christian leaders to build biblically functioning churches that reach increasing numbers of unchurched people, not just with innovations from Willow Creek Community Church in South Barrington, Illinois, but from any church in the world that has experienced God-given breakthroughs.

WILLOW CREEK CONFERENCES
Each year, thousands of local church leaders, staff and volunteers—from WCA Member Churches and others—attend one of our conferences or training events. Conferences offered on the Willow Creek campus in South Barrington, Illinois, include:

Prevailing Church Conference: Foundational training for staff and volunteers working to build a prevailing local church.

Prevailing Church Workshops: More than fifty strategic, day-long workshops covering seven topic areas that represent key characteristics of a prevailing church; offered twice each year.

Promiseland Conference: Children's ministries; infant through fifth grade.

Student Ministries Conference: Junior and senior high ministries.

Willow Creek Arts Conference: Vision and training for Christian artists using their gifts in the ministries of local churches.

Leadership Summit: Envisioning and equipping Christians with leadership gifts and responsibilities; broadcast live via satellite to eighteen cities across North America.

Contagious Evangelism Conference: Encouragement and training for churches and church leaders who want to be strategic in reaching lost people for Christ.

Small Groups Conference: Exploring how developing a church *of* small groups can play a vital role in developing authentic Christian community that leads to spiritual transformation.

To find out more about WCA conferences, visit our website at www.willowcreek.com.

PREVAILING CHURCH REGIONAL WORKSHOPS
Each year the WCA team leads several, two-day training events in select cities across the United States. Some twenty day-long workshops are offered in topic areas including leadership, next-

generation ministries, small groups, arts and worship, evangelism, spiritual gifts, financial stewardship, and spiritual formation. These events make quality training more accessible and affordable to larger groups of staff and volunteers.

To find out more about Prevailing Church Regional Workshops, visit our website at www.willowcreek.com.

WILLOW CREEK RESOURCES™

Churches can look to Willow Creek Resources™ for a trusted channel of ministry tools in areas of leadership, evangelism, spiritual gifts, small groups, drama, contemporary music, financial stewardship, spiritual transformation, and more. For ordering information, call (800) 570-9812 or visit our website at www.willowcreek.com.

WCA MEMBERSHIP

Membership in the Willow Creek Association as well as attendance at WCA Conferences is for churches, ministries, and leaders who hold to a historic, orthodox understanding of biblical Christianity. The annual church membership fee of $249 provides substantial discounts for your entire team on all conferences and Willow Creek Resources, networking opportunities with other outreach-oriented churches, a bimonthly newsletter, a subscription to the *Defining Moments* monthly audio journal for leaders, and more.

To find out more about WCA membership, visit our website at www.willowcreek.com.

WILLOWNET (WWW.WILLOWCREEK.COM)

This Internet resource service provides access to hundreds of Willow Creek messages, drama scripts, songs, videos, and multimedia ideas. The system allows you to sort through these elements and download them for a fee.

Our website also provides detailed information on the Willow Creek Association, Willow Creek Community Church, WCA membership, conferences, training events, resources, and more.

WILLOWCHARTS.COM (WWW.WILLOWCHARTS.COM)

Designed for local church worship leaders and musicians, WillowCharts.com provides online access to hundreds of music charts and chart components, including choir, orchestral, and horn sections, as well as rehearsal tracks and video streaming of Willow Creek Community Church performances.

THE NET (HTTP://STUDENTMINISTRY.WILLOWCREEK.COM)

The NET is an online training and resource center designed by and for student ministry leaders. It provides an inside look at the structure, vision, and mission of prevailing student ministries from around the world. The NET gives leaders access to complete programming elements, including message outlines, dramas, small group questions, and more. An indispensable resource and networking tool for prevailing student ministry leaders!

CONTACT THE WILLOW CREEK ASSOCIATION

If you have comments or questions, or would like to find out more about WCA events or resources, please contact us:

Willow Creek Association
P.O. Box 3188, Barrington, IL 60011-3188
Phone: (800) 570-9812 or (847) 765-0070
Fax: (888) 922-0035 or (847) 765-5046
Web: www.willowcreek.com

TOUGH QUESTIONS

Garry Poole and Judson Poling

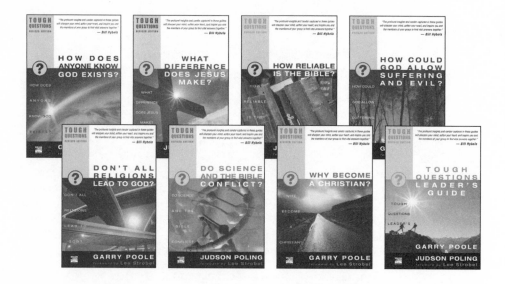

"The profound insights and candor captured in these guides will sharpen your mind, soften your heart, and inspire you and the members of your group to find vital answers together."   —Bill Hybels

This second edition of Tough Questions, designed for use in any small group setting, is ideal for use in seeker small groups. Based on more than five years of field-tested feedback, extensive revisions make this best-selling series easier to use and more appealing than ever for both participants and group leaders.

Softcover

How Does Anyone Know God Exists?	ISBN 0-310-24502-8
What Difference Does Jesus Make?	ISBN 0-310-24503-6
How Reliable Is the Bible?	ISBN 0-310-24504-4
How Could God Allow Suffering and Evil?	ISBN 0-310-24505-2
Don't All Religions Lead to God?	ISBN 0-310-24506-0
Do Science and the Bible Conflict?	ISBN 0-310-24507-9
Why Become a Christian?	ISBN 0-310-24508-7
Leader's Guide	ISBN 0-310-24509-5

Pick up a copy at your favorite local bookstore today!

WILLOW CREEK RESOURCES

ZONDERVAN™

GRAND RAPIDS, MICHIGAN 49530 USA

WWW.ZONDERVAN.COM